# Little Me

# Little Me

by

**Joyce Fielding**

CENTRAL PUBLISHING SERVICES.
**West Yorkshire**

**Paperback ISBN 1-904908-09-8**

**Produced
by**

Central Publishing Services
Royd Street Offices
Milnsbridge
Huddersfield
West Yorkshire
HD3 4QY

**www.centralpublishing.co.uk**

*This book was written for my three lovely children,*

*Robert, Hilary, and Mark Fielding.*

*JF*

# Little Me

## CHAPTER ONE

If she didn't go to the pub with my dad, on warm summer evenings my mother would stand at the front door of our terraced house, chatting to the other women who lived up our street. Apart from the ones who had gone for a bath to Belper Street Public Baths, they would stand on their doorsteps, or sit on their windowsills, some still wearing their black brats and clogs they'd worn all day while working in the winding or weaving sheds of Swallow Street Mill, the huge grey stone building that overshadowed the tiny houses surrounding it, soaking up most of the lives of the people who lived in them.

This get together was their way of getting some fresh air into their lungs, although they all smoked as vigorously as the chimneys surrounding them.

Me and my friend Letty stood with them, listening and learning things we shouldn't. Florrie across at number seven would shout, 'shut your ears you young uns, this isn't for eleven year olds.'

Eleven years old! Where had I been until then? I can't ever remember being a child, just a small person. When I was born on that snowy January morning in 1935, at Springfield Maternity Home, at the top of Preston New Road, struggling into the cold world, while Bing Crosby sang 'June in January' over the radio to my poor mother Annie, who was terrified what was happening to her, and had worked in the mill up to the day before – I realize, at that time, and for the cold months following my introduction to the world, someone must have tended me. Perhaps it was my mother.

On one of my listening in sessions, I learned that she hadn't had the tram fare to get to the nursing home, and at the start of her labour had walked there in the snow, and during her time there, had felt ashamed when the nurses noticed her finger turning green, due to the curtain ring she wore as a wedding ring, due to her own ring being in the pawn shop that week.

'I jumped on and off chairs 'till I was nearly gormless trying to get rid of that one,' she would tell the neighbours, pointing at me. The would laugh, and say to me, 'Never mind cock, you're still here!'

Being one of eight children, she might well have had some experience in child care of sorts, and although she didn't want me, or love me, perhaps she did her best to care for me during those early days.

Annie, a child of her time, at a very early age, had followed the older members of her family to the forbidding Victorian building, the overcrowded Roman Catholic School. The dark interior adorned with figures, pictures, and words of 'thou shalt nots'. Children were admitted to schools at a very tender age then. Parents glad to get them off their hands. Also in winter school was warmer than home. Coal fires cost money!

Playgroups and creches waited for the next generations, not Annie's. She learned what was dished out to her, with little incentive to be anything but what she was, and to be grateful for it, for that's what the R.C Fathers of the Church told her she should be.

Dark haired, blue eyed and very beautiful, at 14yrs, every potential having been left untapped, Annie left school and did what was expected of her, joining the throngs who trailed

through the large black gates of Swallow Street Mill at 7.30 a.m each day of every season, into the sunless sheds, to wind or weave the cotton. It would never have crossed her innocent mind to have dared to ask her 'betters' if there was another option open to her. Two years later, when she met dashing, handsome, and daring young Tom, from Florence Street, and quickly became pregnant, she truly believed the fathers were right – she was a sinner! A few weeks after her trauma and disgrace when the family found out she was pregnant, she recovered from the hiding her dad had given her at the time, and arrangements were made for her to be married to Tom, at the Registry Office in King Street, with much disapproval from his family.

On the day of her wedding, having to have asked for a day off work, without pay, from the mill, she borrowed a pink loose fitting coat from a friend, a few sizes larger than her small self, so as to cover her bump, and with her older sister as her only companion, they walked through the back streets together.

In front of the handful of persons present, she promised to marry Tom for life, and so started her long years in a most miserable marriage.

Tom wasn't all that keen on getting married. At eighteen, he would rather have hung around with the lads, tinkering with their motorbikes on the street corners, staying out till all hours, and chatting up the girls. His apprenticeship with Dutton's Brewery as an interior decorator was only half way through.

On the day he reluctantly met Annie at the Registrars to tie the knot, he would have gone through with it anyway, just to defy his parents, who had suggested he should remain single, and 'pay to her' instead.

He would have defied his stepfather on any count, hating him all through his childhood for having stepped in to live with his mother Emily, when his own father, Herbert, left her, along with himself and his younger sister Irene.

A year before Tom was born his stepfather had been best man at Emily and Herbert's wedding, that had taken place at the Weslyan Chapel, in Harwood Street. Perhaps because Tom looked so much like his father, or perhaps because he was high spirited, and retaliated against any discipline, caused the dislike between the two of them. It was rumoured in the family, in hushed tones, that young Tom had taken a knife to him during one of their arguments.

Emily had produced another brother and sister for Tom, who distanced himself even further, and ignored his stepfather for much the rest of his life. He shut his ears to the doctrines, philosophies, and religious opinions this self taught bookworm tried to force upon him. Although a gentle person, he failed at any fatherly attempt to gain love or respect from the boy who had been named after him – Tom.

And so Annie and Tom got me, and I got them! They say you choose your own parents. I don't think so!

I always think it's a pity that you can't remember what went on in your life before you were three years old. Perhaps in some cases it's best not to know. You rely on photos, and stories about yourself from older, and all kinds of people. I have a friend who swears she remembers her father coming to see her on the day she was born, and vividly describes the tweed jacket he was wearing. Nothing like that ever happened to me.

I would have liked to remember my christening. They tell me I was going to be called Catherine, but an old fellow by the name of Tommy Joyce, who lived near us, up Poplar Street; said to my dad, who he shared a pint with in the Seventrees Working Men's Club, 'What are tha going to call that new babby of thine?' 'Catherine,' my dad told him. 'Well, if tha calls it Joyce, I'll give thee five bob!' So that was it! Joyce!

Like most babies belonging to the working class, I would have been passed around a lot, but it was to be my dad's mother who would move away and take me to live with her during the war years, and who would teach me some of the better things in life, but I did not know that then.

## CHAPTER TWO

My mother's family had moved from Snape Street to Florence Street about the time when I was born, into a house with an extra room. It was not a good situation for these two families to be so close, and the family feuding continued.

Annie and Tom had no choice but to live with them, depositing me on her mother. One more addition to the family would have made little difference, and Annie went back to her job in the mill.

My survival relied on my young mother and her family. Between them, I would have been given milk in a bottle to drink, food, probably from their own plates at mealtimes. I would be washed in the cold grey slopstone in the kitchen, no doubt in the same water used by other members of the family, as hot water was scarce, having to be boiled up on the fire hob, or the gas ring. A penny put in the gas meter did not go far with a big family. I suppose I had nappies; later, knickers, but like all small babies, I would be held out over a newspaper to pooh! thus saving a nappie, and more washing. After I'd 'performed,' it would be rolled up into a newspaper, and burnt in the huge blackleaded firegrate. I might have had a cot, but it was more likely I shared a bed, even the bottom of a bed with others. During the day, along with other babies being minded, and there were always plenty, I would be put outside at the front door. Babies were put out in those days, and people stopped to talk to them, rock the pram if the baby was crying, sit them up if they'd fallen sideways, or put their dummy back in their mouth.

Some years later, the women of the street told me a story of when I was a baby. Of the time I was put out in my big brown pram, that seemingly didn't have a brake, and had been used by a lot of babies in our street. In it, there was an old cushion for me to sit on, (no mention of pillows or bedding) I rocked the pram, and it ran down the street, across the main road at the bottom, known as Cob Wall, and overturned. The cushion was thrown out first, and I landed on top of it!

'You were a lucky little sod,' they told me.

I would not remember how poor we were, the unsanitary conditions, who I slept among, what I ate, how I was dressed, or even know then: how hard it was for a large family, with very little money, to maintain any standards at all. In two short years I must have acquired a strong immunity to disease, cold, poor diet, and life itself….

Then I became a small person.

When I could walk and find my way to my other grandmas, my dad's mother's house, I adopted two homes, going from one to another. As the houses were only ten doors from each other and on the same side of the street, this was easy for me.

Uninvited, I would walk in to the homes of most of our neighbours, where I would get a sweet or a biscuit, even something to take home, if it was baking day.

It would be assumed if a child was missing for a time, that it would be in somebody's house, being watched over.

I only remember my parents and grandparents vaguely in those young years, but it was on my dad's mother's doorstep that I would wait for Mr. Smith, the ice cream man, to call.

Mr. Smith, the 'stop me and buy one' ice cream man, came down our street two or three times a week. As soon as he turned the corner, I would spot him at once, riding his bike, the little white cart on wheels attached to the front. Bottles of thick red raspberry sauce balanced on top, while inside contained the rich creamy vanilla ice cream, all ready to be scooped out with a big silver scoop, into a large biscuit cone, just for me. I exchanged it for the penny I'd been holding in my small sticky hand for a very long time, as I sat on my grandma's doorstep waiting for him.

'That's a special one just for you,' he'd say. And I thought it was.

I've been told I would sit for hours waiting for the first glimpse of him. When I saw him, I would run into my grandma's house, screaming with delight, 'Smiffs here! Smiffs here!'

If one of your first memories is of ice cream, I wonder what psychologists would make of it?

Whatever! I have loved it ever since.

Florence Street, a street like many other streets in Blackburn. A street for ordinary folk. Where on Friday nights rents were collected by the rent collector. A penny a week on life insurance was collected by 'the man from the prudential'. Sixpence pence was set aside for the clothing club, and the milkman was paid if he was lucky.

In this long treeless corridor of small houses, standing side by side like toy soldiers in a row, little chimneys perched on top bellowed smoke and smut, trying to compete with the chimneys of the mills and the foundries around them. Men had returned to these homes after the first world war, sure in the belief that an Englishman's home was his castle, with no desire to ever move away again.

It was usual to be born and die in these streets. Perhaps when the younger ones got wed, they would move a street or two away, but never far. If anyone went to live a tram ride away, they might as well have emigrated.

Postage stamp sized backyards at the back of each house, contained various things that families thought important. Ours contained my dad's motorbike, along with coal stacked up in a corner, and like everybody else our long tin bath hung on a hook on the wall near to the back door. On a windy night it was bedlam listening to the baths clatter against the walls. On Friday nights, baths were taken in, placed by the fire, and filled with hot water, that had been boiling up for ages in numerous pans and kettles, before members of the family took their turn to have a bath, while the others, already bathed, or waiting, went upstairs or into the parlour.

The privy was at the bottom of the yard next to the back gate. We kept ours locked at night, because a woman further down the street had visited her lav' before she went to bed, pulled down her knickers, sat down, and sat on a fellow's knee! He'd gone in there to shelter out of the rain, they said.

On a dark night people went in pairs. You could guide yourself down there by holding the washing line, but if you were a bit scared of the dark, it was nice to have somebody stand outside of the door. You could hear the person next door on their lav' at the same time you sat on yours. The lady next door would shout to me, 'Hello little Joyce! Are you alright?'

So, for my first three years I lived in Florence Street, where the younger set went off to the mills every morning.

The sound of their black clogs rang out on the stone flagged pavements, before the shrill sound of the 'blower' pierced through the morning air, at 7.25 a.m prompt, warning them to hurry, or they would be quartered – 15 minutes docked from their wages, if they 'clocked' in after 7.30 a.m.

A cloud of silence enveloped the streets as the prison like mill gates clanged behind them. When the crowds had gone, my dad drove off to work on his motorbike. Always a good worker, he unleashed his artistic abilities painting and decorating the local pubs and hotels in the area, sampling the different ales the landlords offered at the same time.

Each weekday was much of a muchness. For the older women, working at home was just as hard as labouring in the weaving sheds. Trying to make ends meet would be left to them, as wages earned on Fridays were usually gone by Monday. Monday morning for some of them, was spent taking shoes, suits, wedding rings, and even bedding ,to the Pawn Broker, or asking the grocer for a few bits on tick until the weekend . Some took in washing, as well as looking after the babies in the family, or any babies who needed minding.

All during my childhood, weekends seemed to me, two days given by God, for Catholics to have time to go to church, and everybody else to have two days to get ready to go back to work on Monday.

On Friday night, children were sent to the Pawn Brokers, exchanging the dockets and money to redeem the goods their mothers had traded at the start of the week. Dad's shoes, and suits would be placed back on the hangers behind the bedroom doors. In most cases, the dads never having missed them.

Women of the streets were very secretive were men were concerned!

Friday was chip night! A quick tea, because there was a lot to do. Not fish and chips, not for the children anyway. Fish was too expensive, only dads got a fish.

Friday night was dad's night out. They never took their wives out on Friday night, but joined their mates, or met their 'fancy women'. But Saturday night, the wives were privileged to join them in the pubs. The wives deserved their Saturday night out!

Saturday morning, Florence Street, like others in the district, was a hive of activity. Everyone seemed to be in a good mood on Saturdays. Front doorsteps and windowsills were scrubbed and stoned at the edges with a cream stone. A usual shout of 'I'll do your step for you, luv,' could be heard from one neighbour to another, if one was pregnant, or elderly. Many went down to Blackburn Market on Saturday afternoon. A fine colourful market, with numerous stalls, selling anything and everything, covered over with black and green tarpaulin that held the rain in wet weather, and dripped onto your head, as you dodged between them. Tripe, black puddings, oat cakes and a bit of boiled ham for Sunday tea, could be bought there.

A jelly made on Saturday evening, was put in a dish, covered with a plate, and placed outside on the windowsill. It would be left until Sunday, to eat at teatime with custard, after the ham salad. Nobody touched or took away those jellies. All different colours and flavours, they sat on the newly cream stoned windowsills, setting dutifully until the Sabbath.

The local pubs opened their doors, and by eight – o – clock in the evening the men started to fill the bars and the tap rooms. The wives would follow them in little groups later.

Husbands and wives never seemed to walk to the pubs together. It was like a ritual. I remember a few years later, my mother's mother always wearing the same white blouse that she saved specially for Saturday night, and combing her long black hair back into a tidy bun, to go on her only outing of the week. She called for the other wives in the street, and they walked together slowly, arm in arm, chatting, until they reached the door of this smokey little place, where they could 'let their hair down' for an hour or two, as they made their way to the 'snug', a room where women were allowed, and sat themselves on the same seats, and ordered the same drinks, usually Guinness or Pale Ale, as they did every Saturday night.

Their children, not ready to go to bed, would sit on the pub doorstep or on the flagstones outside. They'd shout messages to their mothers inside – 'Mam, buy us a bottle of Tizer,' or, 'Mam, can we have some more crisps?'

They really laid it on thick, and milked their mothers for all they were worth. To keep them quiet, and glad to get away from them for an hour or two, bottles of pop, crisps and nuts would be brought out to them from time to time, and an eye kept on them all through the large open pub door. The wafting smell from the inside, of beer, meat pies, smoke, cheap perfume and Brylcream was comforting, as the children became more tired and fractious.· They stood on the windowsills and peered at their parents through frosted glass windows.

As the night darkened, those inside would start to sing, and the children outside would start to fight, shout, cry, and become cold and wet if it was raining, until some member of their family, usually an Auntie, would come out and take them home, putting them to bed ( a wash would do in the morning) before she returned to the pub.

Throwing out time came to soon, as the landlord closed his pub doors on the people he knew so well, and renderings of 'Danny Boy' would echo along the streets, mingling with couples quarrelling, and later, wives screaming, as the wife beaters vented their feelings, about work, money, someone kissing someone they shouldn't have, or whatever, upon their poor suffering spouses.

My father's parents did not frequent the pub, as they did not drink, as such. Perhaps the odd Sherry at Christmas, or glass of wine for a birthday. So I suppose on most weekends I was handed over to them. I would be spoiled a little bit, and given nice things to eat, and maybe a glass of sarsaparilla, that grandma would pour out of the huge stone bottle, that she kept outside in the backyard, to keep it cool. When the sarsaparilla was all finished, she kept the stone jar, and during the cold weather, she filled it with hot water, and we had them in our beds as water bottles. They made a heck of a noise if they dropped out of bed in the night. It was at these times I stayed with her, that she must have made my little dresses for me. I don't think she was much of a seamstress, and never pretended to be, but like most housewives then, she could put simple things together, and could quickly stitch up a dress for me, out of a piece of Miss Muffet print bought from the market.

During these weekends, I would miss the family rows in my mother's home. The shouting, the fighting, the 'throwing out'. Luckily, I was oblivious to it all, and escaped the awful trauma of the experience of seeing families beating each other up, until a few years later, at least.

# CHAPTER THREE

I did a lot of sitting on doorsteps, doing nothing – just thinking – alone with my small thoughts and feelings. If I'd have known when I was three, that going to school meant being there most days of my life for the next twelve years, I would have sat on my grandma's doorstep a bit longer, instead of wanting to be with the other children.

I never expected, or felt neglected at not being taken to school by a grown up. If I cried on my first morning, nobody would have bothered much – but I shouldn't think I did. Even then I was fairly independent, and had started to look after myself, and have done ever since. If anyone has been over kind to me, or said they wanted to take care of me, or even later in life, said they loved me – I've been very moved, and for a while may have responded by going overboard for them, if they were male, but only ever half believed them.

It was my turn to enter Moss Street School, where my dad and his brother and two sisters had gone before me. My name had been put down when I was born. So at Easter 1938, I followed the other children up Florence Street, round the corner into Moss Street, and into the 'Babies' class.

A Church of England School, and because it was nearer to our house than St. Albans, I was lucky not to have come under the doctrine of the Roman Catholic Church, as my mother was still a catholic, and no way would have been allowed to change her religion to marry.

Little ones from large families soon become 'one of the gang', and during the next four seasons, I went with the other children from the streets, to school.

We wore old socks on our cold red hands in the winter, and I wore a pair of black boots on my feet. I remember these, as they were too big, and probably handed down to me from my mother's younger brother, who was about four years older than myself.

Sharp memories come to me, of having chewing gum in my hair, and a kind teacher cutting it out, and during the warmer months, having gas tar on my fingers and legs, as well as stuck to the bottom of my sandals. When the weather was very hot, our streets were full of gas tar, and a favourite pastime was to sit on the kerb and prod the bubbles it produced with a stick.

In the large school hall, my class was separated from the other classes in there with a dusty maroon coloured velvet curtain. I soon learned to sit up straight, put my hands on my head if we were making too much noise, stand still in the playground when the teacher blew the whistle, and to walk in to the school without speaking, when she blew it again. The babies were allowed in first. I hammered pegs into little holes, threaded large beads onto tape, put pieces of wooden jig saws together, and learned to keep my hands clean by washing them in a tiny sink, that had hot and cold running water taps, and a small bar of pink soap, that we all shared. My very own towel was hung on my very own peg, just under the huge mirror on the wall. I don't know now if it had a fish or some animal printed on it, but I knew it was *mine*, and nobody else had to use it. I loved this part of the day, placing the little black plug into the sink, turning the taps on and off, and sinking my small hands into the lovely clear water. I learned to take my place in a queue for milk at playtime, learned to say 'toilet' instead of 'lavvy', and to put my hand up in the air when I wanted to go there, when a 'big girl' out of the next class would take me. Toilets were in the playground yard, and babies were not allowed to go on their own, in case they got lost.

We all put our wet shoes and socks on the large mesh fireguard that surrounded the coke stove in the hall, when we arrived cold and wet on rainy mornings.

I learned to sing 'Ten Green Bottles Hanging on a Wall, and all the nursery rhymes, that never did make a lot of sense to me. My letters (alphabet) I almost knew, because my grandma had taught me, as well as my numbers up to ten. I learned to say the prayer - 'Thank you for the world so sweet', with my eyes closed right to the very end, and to mumble and jumble my way through 'The Lord's Prayer' with words that even the Lord himself would not have recognised. Most of all I learned to look after little me, and in time to become fairly 'street wise'!

I would think some of the teachers would have known my dad, and his brother and sisters, as they had been there not many years before me. They would have been fairly well behaved children, and pretty knowledgeable, due to my grandma's teachings, as during her teenage years, she had wanted to be a governess, but circumstances dictated she went into the mills. At least her children, and myself, benefited and became literate at an early age. It seems my dad was a bit of a scallywag at the school, but as he was in the school football team, he would have been quite popular.

Just after nine-o-clock each morning, when we were safely assembled in class, the register would be called, just like it had been in schools for over a century. We sat behind our wooden desks, and said, 'Yes Miss' when the teacher called our name. When this was completed, she would close the pages, stand up from her desk, come to the front of the class, look at us, and choose one of us to take the register to the headmaster's office. My grandma told me later, it was the fear of my life at the time. I'm reported to have pleaded with her. 'Please! Grandma, tell the teacher I don't want to take the register. Please ask her not to choose me.' It was supposed to be an honour to be chosen, and I had been selected a few times, and hated it.

I'd carried the big blue book out of the class, through the hall, and down the long dark corridor to the headmaster's office. I had to knock on the door, and when his big voice boomed 'Come in!' I had to place the register on the floor, and put my hands around the huge doorknob of the massive wooden door to open it. When it opened, into the high ceiling, musty, dimly lit and forbidding room, full of the largest chairs I had ever seen, and books round all the walls, I picked up the big blue book again, and walked over to his desk, that was higher than my head, and placed it down on the pile of others already there. This man with beady eyes, and spectacles on the end of his nose, didn't look up, or even say 'thank you'.

It became a nightmare for me, and I worried my grandma with it every day for a while, as it was no good telling my mother. I didn't bother her with problems, then, or ever. But I do remember what my grandma told me – a saying she repeated to me many times as I grew up, and the same words I've said to myself over the years, 'Don't be silly, - he's only a man with a nose on!' These words got me through many an ordeal in life, giving me the confidence that was instilled into me so young.

Much later, when grown up, I became a 'school matron' for a time, at a private school, and each morning I would go into the headmaster's study, to discuss with him, my boy boarders, and the events of the school!

While I was worrying about taking the register to the headmaster, families around me were worrying about more important things, to them anyway. Mothers worried about the school inspector calling, when they kept their older children away from school for maybe weeks at a time, for various reasons. The main one being to look after the toddlers in the family, while the mother gave birth yet again. Parents could be prosecuted by the attendance board, but they took little notice of this threat. Sometimes a letter would be sent to school explaining an absence, but a lot of the mothers couldn't write well enough to string a letter together.

Children would stay at home because they had no shoes, a regular excuse. They would receive a letter from the school, saying, 'Having no shoes is no reason not to attend school!' A 'shoe fund' was set up in most schools in poorer areas, each child paying into it a penny a week; then if needs must, a second hand pair of shoes or boots would be found for them. That, and another penny for the 'penny bank' on Monday mornings, made a dent in the housekeeping of the larger families. 'Tell your teacher, we're not bloody millionaires!' was heard frequently.

Sadly, some children stayed at home, and in some cases, never returned, illnesses of the time, taking their short lives away. Measles and childhood diseases, along with scabies, impetigo, chilblains, lice, ringworm and scabs, could be treated, and the child home nursed, with perhaps the one visit from the doctor. But a visit cost three shillings, sometimes the doctor being paid, sometimes not. Grandmothers handed down their home remedies. Glycerine and lemon was made up for coughs, and a steam kettle kept boiling in the sickroom if a 'Friar's Balsam' inhaler wasn't on hand. Bread poultices for boils. Chilblains were bathed in hot brine that had been used for pickling beef or tongues. Syrups of Figs was given out on Friday nights, and a stocking, dipped in bacon fat, dripping or goose grease, was worn round the neck to ward off colds. It was usual to see the miners going off to work with a stocking or small scarf, dipped in the grease, wrapped round their necks.

Invalid diets consisted of 'pobs'. This was bread, broken into pieces, placed in a bowl, covered with hot milk, and sprinkled with sugar. Boiled tripe, Calf's Foot Jelly, egg in milk, gruel, barley water, onion soup, homemade lemonade, and treacle toffee were the favourite things given to the invalids, and supplied by the neighbours. Everyone would rally round, and pop in and out of your house, bringing things to eat, offering to do the washing or shopping, and of course, would stone your front step and windowsill on Friday night!

It was the more serious illnesses – bronchitis, scarlet fever, diphtheria, and rheumatic fever, children fought for their lives with. The local fever hospital coped, the wards at times overflowing, their patients kept in isolation, and families divided, not being able to visit, for fear of the risk of the infections being spread. The only way they saw their children, was to see them through the ward windows, and the heartache must have torn at them, as they wanted to cradle their little ones in their arms as they lay so ill, or dying.

Sanitary inspectors frequented the school often, and

sometimes we were given a holiday for as long as three weeks, while walls were washed and fumigation carried out.

In the meantime, I was becoming more knowing about the every day world. I now knew about the ruler, or cane! I knew punishment was given for tearing books, stealing chalk, talking in lines, banging desk lids, and ringing door bells, if reported.

'Keep your nose clean,' said my grandma. That meant a lot of things!

So I did!

I was becoming useful, and could even go to the corner shop on my own. I was probably sent to buy a penny cream stone or a dolly blue, if it was washday, or a packet of biscuits, or perhaps I went to buy something for myself.

Mrs Eatough's shop sold everything under the sun, but was a toffee shop really. This tiny grey haired woman, with eyes twinkling through her rimless spectacles, could oblige you with most things from her Alladin's cave. It was packed to capacity. Large bottles of sweets, in the most amazing colours, stood on the high shelves. The floor was cluttered with soap, firelights, parrafin, and most things you could mention for needs in the home. While at the window, I would gaze for ages, at the deep black spanish, in the shape of smoking pipes, filled with red hundred and thousands, and pin wheels with an all day sucker in the centre. Creamy brown Holland Toffee in a tray, all broken up into eatable size pieces, with a small hammer. Coltsfoot rock, Nestle's milky bars, Crunchies, Smarties, and Barley Sugars for my grandma, that I never went much on.

Some of the window was taken up with homemade meat pies, and little fairy cakes, with silver balls on. The shop door bell tinkled as you walked in, and the smell that met you, was warm and delicious. All this mingled with the rich tobacco smell of Mr. Eatough's pipe that he smoke continuously. I loved going to Mrs. Eatoughs. It was cosy, warm, and secure. It was a place to linger in, even if you had only a halfpenny to spend.

Had I been told my grandma was moving from Florence Street? Did I feel anything? Was I upset? Did I cry? Did she say 'Goodbye' to me? I don't know. The memory hasn't lingered. All I remember is that suddenly she had gone. She had moved away, with my grandad, and the rest of her family, to Haston Lea Avenue, into a semi detached council house, at the north end of the town. The district was called Brownhill, near to the countryside. She must have thought she was in heaven to have had a modern house, with a bathroom, three bedrooms, and a garden front and back.

It cannot have been much longer after their exodus from the back street, that I was to follow them.

One Sunday morning I was taken to visit them by my mother's father! Now, I wouldn't have called Jim a grandfatherly type at all. His maternal instincts, from what I heard about him later on, was that he was all mouth and fists. Neither do I remember him speaking to me in all the ten years I happened to know him. However, he took me to see my grandma, and the story goes… She thought I was being neglected, and told me many years later, that I was so sore under my arms, round my neck and in between my legs, that she offered to have me for a couple of days – her intention to get me better. It was probably 'opening time', so Jim agreed I could stay, and left me there – where I stayed for seven years!

## CHAPTER FOUR

From that fateful Sunday morning, my life was axed.

Goodbye Florence Street, Goodbye Annie and Tom, Goodbye Moss Street School, and Goodbye to Mrs Eatough, to my wonderful Mr.'Smiff', and all the neighbours who knew me.

Did they miss me? Want me back? Enquire if I was alright? or even noticed I'd gone? I was still my mother's only child, but as I started my new life, I did not see her again for another year.

Did I miss them? I don't think so!

I was now in a world were I had clean knickers every day, a vest, liberty bodice, and a chemise made by my grandma, trimmed round the hem with white cotton lace. I wore neat Miss Muffet print dresses, with knitted cardigans, where each day, grandma pinned a clean handkerchief, after she'd dabbed it with eucalyptus oil. My warm outdoor coat and wool pixie hat were my very own, not handed down, and my shoes fit.

I played in the garden on the soft green grass, paying little heed to the large hole being dug there, waiting to accommodate the Anderson air raid shelter we were going to spend our nights in during the months to come.

While I revelled in a daily bath of bubbles, and slept in my own single bed, I did not know my grandma was unhappy, because there was a threat of war looming, and a lot of lives were going to change. Her teenage years had been clouded by the first world war, and now the dread of a second one so soon after, made her fearful of the consequences. In those awful years, grandad had been gassed in the trenches in France, and shipped home to England in 1917, along with Herbert, his best friend, my dad's father, both with frostbite in their feet. Grandad was gravely concerned, keeping his thoughts and memories to himself, so as not to upset his family.

Blackout material was bought to cover the windows, the Anderson shelter installed, and grown ups talked of food rationing. The larder was stocked with tea, coffee, tinned fruit, chocolate, and carnation milk.

In the meantime – oblivious to any danger – I started to attend a new school.

Roe Lea School was modern, surrounded by playing fields. A long walk from home, I trailed to it every morning with a group of local children, willingly or not. I felt no traumas there that I can remember. No one was asked to take the big blue register to the headmaster. There was no shoe fund, but I still took my penny for the penny bank on Monday mornings. We could buy a small tube of creamy Horlicks, or malty Ovaltine tablets from the teacher, at playtime. My grandma made me up a picnic lunch, that I took in a special box with my name on, as the walk was too far to go home between 12 and 1.p.m.   I carried a special cloth bag with my initials embroidered on, that contained my 'pumps' on the days we did drill. I drank my daily bottle of milk, that was supplied to us free, and I drank everybody elses who didn't want theirs. I now had a red copy book for writing practise and spelling, and I could read very well.

My new friend, June, lived a few doors higher up the hill from us. She had blonde curly hair that I was very envious of.

I ate my crusts, but it didn't make any difference. I had straight dark hair, cut short to add insult to injury, and washed every Friday night with black antiseptic smelling – Derbac soap. 'It keeps the nits away,' said my grandma. It must have done, as I never had a nit all the time I lived with her, but I certainly made up for it later!

Once, there was an atmosphere in the house.

I started very early in my life to be sensitive to atmosphere, and have never been able to cope with people who couldn't waken up in the same mood each morning. Walking on eggshells, wondering what people are going to say or do, I could never tolerate. Yet little did I know when sensing the atmosphere that time at my grandma's, that it was anything to do with me – but it was!

Grandad was agitated, I could tell by the sound of his voice, as he firmly stated his view about something to my grandma, who answered with very little response.

I had a rag doll with a celluloid face. She was not a doll that I held dear. I called her Bubbles, because that name was on a label, stitched to the back of her neck. My friend June had a small black pot pickaninny doll – and- we'd swapped dolls! June was happy. I was happy. Grandad was not happy!

I came to know him as a free thinker, but not then. The word racist, atheist, and such, were far ahead in my vocabulary, but I do know my grandma took the black doll back to June's house, and came back with Bubbles. Nothing more was ever said about it.

My bedroom, overlooking the back garden, was shared with my Auntie Eva. She was pretty witty and bright, with beautiful curly auburn hair, and, ten years older than me.

About to leave Bangor Street Girl's School, where I was to follow her in eight years from then, she was excited about going to work, that she found in a lovely gown shop, in the arcade, in the middle of town. She made me clean my teeth before I went to bed at night, with my own toothbrush, and toothpaste in a little red tin. When it was new, the cake of toothpaste was wrapped in red cellophane paper. I would unwrap it carefully, so that I could peer through it, and my world would be seen through a rosy glow.

She made me brush my hair, and she rinsed it in vinegar on Fridays, to make it shine.

We were both blessed with lovely singing voices, and were encouraged to sing. This we did in our beds at night, before we said our prayers. We sang 'Alice Blue Gown' 'You are My Heart's Delight' 'How Deep is the Ocean', and Eva sang 'This is my Lovely Day' and songs from the operas I did not know.

Grandma sang as she pottered about doing her housework. 'Goodbye Dolly I Must Leave You' 'We'll Meet again' 'Keep the Home Fires Burning' are songs I remember, and all the Richard Tauber melodies. She never sang 'Sally' or any of the songs Gracie Fields sang. Grandma said Gracie Fields had a voice like a corncrate, and what ever a corncrate was, I thought so as well.

As my dad had married Annie, and his younger sister Irene had also flown the nest early, after leaving Blackburn High School, and blossoming into a good looking, self confident woman, who could sing and play the piano well, and always seemed to know what she wanted in life, my grandma must have prayed that the armed services would not claim her younger children, Frank and Eva if war was declared. But it was summer. Everyone was enjoying themselves. Maybe war would not come.

I was becoming quite refined. Grandma told me – Nice ladies don't smoke or swear. Well dressed people wear gloves and clean shoes. She taught me to look for the beautiful things in life that don't cost a penny. – To wonder at the moon, sunrise, sunsets, pictures in the fire, poetry, colours, shapes – and never to visit anyone empty handed!

Strauss waltzes and marches played on her old wind up gramophone were the start of my musical interest. Books, paints, pencils, tracing paper and crayons she bought for me, stimulated the arty side of my brain.

At that time – I was a lucky little girl.

Summer 1939 – When children didn't have inoculations for this, that, and the other. When I contracted 'measles' I'd been lucky enough to had built up a good immunity of my own. I quite enjoyed being nursed in my grandma's big double bed in the front bedroom. Sitting among the large pillows in my cosy pink dressing gown, I was surrounded by tit bits to eat, home made lemonade to drink, and my books, pencils and crayons to occupy my time. When she left me, to go out to the shops, I promised faithfully to stay in bed. I only broke my promise to pop out to look through the diamond shaped panes of the leaded windows, to see if she was coming back. Then I would be rewarded with a huge piece of 'ribbon cake' from the confectioners that was at the bottom of the avenue, near to the tram stop. She brought it upstairs, on a plate, with a special fork – just to eat cake with, and a serviette she'd embroidered with white daisies. I dissected the pieces of lovely springy sponge, all arranged in different colours, and ate them slowly, one by one, while the soft butter cream oozed from the sides.

Life for me, was a happy routine, with only childish problems that little girls encounter. On Friday night, (before hair washing time), grandma and I would walk down the hill to the Newsagent and Sweet shop. It was not the same as Mrs Eatoughs; no shop could ever be the same as that, but the doorbell tinkled, and the lights inside reflected invitingly on the bottles of sweets above my head. Grandma paid the shopkeeper, Mr. Chambers, ( a name I found very amusing, and so did she, as she always gave a sly smile after she'd greeted him) for the weekly newspapers. I would buy my 'Chick's Own' comic, and my usual packet of 'Smarties'. I always got these, as I could 'put lipstick on' with the red ones; then we would choose something for the others at home. Cadbury's chocolate, Crunchie bars and Barley Sugars for grandma, were weighed, and taken home to eat around the fireside.

An only child in the household, I did listen in to adult conversation, sometimes too much. I learned new names – Hitler, Mussolini, Blackshirts, Winston, Mr Chamberlain, and whoever they were, they had become very important, and a great nuisance to me, taking up a lot of time, when I wanted my grandparents to talk of other things. I had to be quiet when the news was on the radio, and not to bother grandad when he was reading the newspaper. Although I was happy, - there was an undercurrent, as I listened and watched their faces in conversation. A feeling of unrest and uncertainty, that I did not understand, hung over us.

But – What did I care? The summer sky was blue and everything around me, warm and gentle. School holidays went on forever it seemed. I'd never really taken to school, and never would. For the rest of my life I would kick against rules that stated I had to be somewhere at a stated time if it meant being in a place I wasn't keen on. The free spirit in me was squashed early, and I was programmed.

But not that summer!

They say the first person a girl falls in love with is her father – Not for me! The first person I fell in love with was my Uncle Frank.

He must have been about sixteen, when I went to live at my grandmas. I don't remember even noticing him before then. He'd left Bangor Street Boy's School, and was also working as an apprentice, along side my dad, at Dutton's Breweries. He was so good to me. We had great fun. He teased me, and chased me round the garden as fast as my little legs would carry me. We had pillow fights, and I laughed and laughed. He was my hero, and it was so easy to fall in love with his handsome good looks, and his lovely smile, as young as I was. At weekends he would take me to visit my grandma's youngest sister, another Eva, my great aunt. She and her husband had a farm up Feniscowles, a district at the other side of town. Her daughter Valerie was my age, and we would swing on the garden gate together, that led to the farmhouse. Great Aunt Eva would give us delicious homemade goodies to eat.

It must have been lovely to have had her for a mother. She smiled all the time, and spoke in a soft voice. She would sit with Valerie and me, under one of the large trees by the barn, and cuddle us. I was fortunate to keep in touch with her, on and off, during her long life. Much later, when I became a student nurse, I was on the ward at the local hospital when her husband died. I hadn't known him very well, he was always at work on his land, but he left her a widow while she was still very young. Sadly, another terrible blow to her life was loosing her only son, (who I'd never known) when he was killed on his motorbike on the eve of his twenty first birthday.

The farm was sold, and Great Aunt Eva and Valerie lived together for the rest of their days.

On my visit to the farm, most of all I liked being with Frank when he lifted me up onto the back of the great farm horse, the biggest animal in the world, or so I thought. Frank walked with us round the field, and I would feel the sharp black hair of the horse on my small legs, and feel her heavy breathing. I was always terrified, but I wouldn't have missed my ride on it for anything.

Frank was always singing. His rich tones echoed through the rooms of the house, and the song he sang most, 'When They Begin the Beguine' always makes me think of him, and feel so close to him. Wherever I have been in my life where music is played, and they ask for requests, I always request it. Even the street busker in my home town now, many years on, plays it for me.

During that summer, I had no doubt that Frank belonged to me, and that someday I would marry him. Like a princess in a book, I would wear a white flowing dress, and have flowers in my hair, which by then, would of course, be long – and curly!

# CHAPTER FIVE

War came!

Not only the changing shadows from autumn to winter, but a darkness invaded us. We were let out of school early, yet dusk had fallen before we got to our homes. The memory of my lovely summer dimmed as I watched the blackout material being placed across the windows, and the Anderson air raid shelter furnished with all kinds of peculiar things. Torches, hot water bottles, blankets, pillows, toilet rolls, and a bucket, - 'That's for you,' grandma told me.

I would see and hear when I grew up, how that war started. I would watch old films, of families sitting around their radios in their living rooms, waiting to hear the fate of the nation. I would hear the address from the then Prime Minister, stating that 'we were at war with Germany.'

But at the time it was really happening, I had no idea at all what it was all about. The Anderson shelter was a cute 'little house' for June and me to play in. I wasn't too keen on the blackout material blocking the windows so early in the evenings, and I couldn't see the point at all when all the street lamps went out, and grandma took me to buy my Smarties with the aid of a torch to light our way. I could have sweets twice a week. I soon became familiar with the little books called 'ration books,' with perforated coupons inside, that had to be given up to shopkeepers in exchange for food.

My dad came to see me one day. I don't know if I

remembered him or not, having not seen him for many months, and not having seen him very much before then. But there he was! He'd come to see me!

'Your daddy is going away,' my grandma told me, 'and he wants you to sing for him.' I vaguely remember standing close to him, while the other members of the family semi circled round us. I sang 'Wish me Luck as you Wave me Goodbye.' Yes, it was a Gracie Fields song, but grandma said I sang it much nicer than she did. My dad had enlisted for the army as soon as he could, glad to get away from the streets for the first time in his life, and to get away from Annie and her family. Being young and adventurous, he'd joined the Bomb Disposal Squad, as a driver. I wasn't to see much of him again for the next few years. Those next few years were the 'time of his life!'

When the sharp sound of the loud piercing siren wailed, rudely interrupting our sleep, there was a scuffling of activity in the kitchen, while grandma grabbed the filled flasks of hot tea, and sandwiches she'd made earlier. I was helped from my little bed, all tired and sleepy, and guided into the garden, down the two small wooden unsteady steps into the Anderson air raid shelter. What seemed a 'cute little house' to play in during the day, had lost its appeal in the cold and pitch black night. Grandma fussed and arranged things, while grandad built the sandbags we'd been provided with, up to the door of the shelter. I slept, apart from the times I had to 'tinkle' in the bucket.

I know they didn't sleep, perhaps nodded for a few moments now and then. They sat - and waited! They sat, helpless, listening to the thud of the bombs dropping on Preston docks, a town a few miles away. They sat, all night sometimes, waiting for the sound of the 'all clear.'

Grandad and Eva had still to go to their work next day. He as a clerk at the Ribble Bus Company, Eva to the gown shop in the arcade.

I haven't mentioned Eva going into the Anderson shelter, because, she didn't go in! 'If I'm going to die; then I'm going to die in my own bed,' she said. Wild horses wouldn't have dragged her in that shelter. I don't think grandad would have left his warm bed either, if grandma hadn't insisted.

One night I was sitting in the shelter, which now was damp and cold, wrapped in a blanket, and reading my 'Chick's Own', with a tiny torch, when grandma started looking over the sandbags, waiting for grandad to join us. He was taking a very long time to come out. 'Tom! Tom!' she kept shouting out into the darkness of the garden, and there he was – he'd gone back into the house for a saucer of milk, to give to a baby hedgehog he'd found, while searchlights lit up the sky, and planes flew overhead. He calmed grandma down, saying, 'Don't worry! The Jerries won't get us. They have our town marked out as a great lake on their maps!' How he knew that, nobody will ever know. But he was right! Blackburn, being a valley was mapped out as a lake by the enemy during the war.

Christmas, that year, quickly came and went, as did birthdays. So quiet, as any celebration of them faded from my memory. But one thing that never faded from my memory was Frank walking out of my life!

He had gone! He didn't even say Goodbye!

Having given his age as one year older than he was, he'd also enlisted. In no time at all, he'd done his squarebashing, and was quickly shipped out to Burma. My grandma held a photo in her hands, and gazed at him, dressed in his new uniform. The army had come as a shock to Frank, and he looked sad, pale, and drawn. With her brown eyes brimming with tears, she said, 'Oh! My little lad! My poor little lad!'

He was still in my heart. I wrote him letters, as best I could. I was still going to marry him!

On the night grandad was late home, grandma was like a 'cat on hot bricks,' The blackouts had been put up at the windows, and she kept going to the front door and peering into the darkness, to see if she could see him coming up the avenue. She risked the cry of the street warden shouting to her to 'get that light out,' as she opened and closed the door; then opened the window blind slightly, as though all this would hasten his return.

After work, he had gone to the doctor's surgery. I don't think he was ill at that time. No doubt he had gone to pick up a prescription for grandma, as these were made up by the doctor in those days. She was starting to suffer with phlebitis, and I remember lots of medication taking space in the kitchen cupboard.

Doctor Edward's surgery was a long way from Brownhill. It was at Little Harwood, near to the war memorial gardens. The sunken gardens were in memory of men from the district, who had fallen during the first world war. There was a beautiful tall clock standing in the midst of the rose beds, designed on the style of 'Big Ben.' The whole of the area was surrounded by iron railings, and huge black gates, decorated with touches of gold. Sometimes when grandma went to see the doctor, I would go with her, and we would stop and rest there for a while, waiting for the clock to chime, while she read the names of the men who had 'fallen.'

I didn't think 'fallen' was so bad! I fell all the time. But I was only five. I didn't understand .

We waited for grandad, who was now very late. I mixed the cocoa in our bedtime beakers. This was one of my jobs, as well as ironing the hankies on 'smoothing' day.

The door knocker wrapped loudly, and grandma rushed to open the door. Eva and me heard her gasp in horror. There was grandad, not looking like grandad at all. His head and face covered with great white bandages. Only his eyes were showing. He looked like the 'invisible man.' Grandma was shocked, and started to ask question after question. Aunt Eva guided him into the kitchen, and sat him on a chair. I screamed and screamed and screamed!

Poor old grandad! The story gradually unfolded. When he could speak properly, or just enough to be understood, he told how he left the doctor' surgery in the blackout, and with the aid of his torchlight, crossed the road to walk by the side of the gardens, on his way to catch the tramcar for home.

Unknown to him, the iron gates and railings had been removed from the gardens during that week, to make bombs with, to fight Hitler. Grandad fell about eight feet into the gardens below, breaking his nose, and cutting himself badly. Some kind people had taken him back into the doctor, who, as grandad described it, patched him up, and arranged for someone with a car to bring him home.

Until he died in his seventies, he had a blue scar on his nose from that terrible night, and the horror of seeing him at the door, swathed in bandages, stayed with me.

Grandma did not 'neighbour,' meaning she did not pop in and out of other people's houses, as women often did in the back streets. I don't remember anyone dropping in for a cup of tea. Her sisters Miriam and Maggie sometimes came to visit for the afternoon. Perhaps grandad didn't like her mixing with the neighbours. Lots of husbands didn't. Women visited each other when 'he' was out. They exchanged confidences, and lent each other a shilling or two, when money was short, or called in with a cake, a few eggs, perhaps a packet of tea, or cast of clothes for the children. If 'he' came in, they didn't stay. It was a world only women knew.

Haston Lea Avenue, being a bit more upper crusty than the streets further down in the town, wouldn't have dreamed of 'neighbouring.' No – 'can you lend me a cup of sugar, luv?' in that road. Grandma passed the time of day, and remarked on the weather with people she passed, or stood next to in the shops, but nothing more. Then one day an incident occurred, that changed our lives yet again. A Hawker came knocking on the front door. He was down and out, gaunt, and probably hungry. He wasn't begging or abusive. He was just trying to earn an honest crust by selling yellow dusters. He wasn't likely to become a tycoon, or be jailed for frauding the banks by doing this. He just wanted enough for a cup of tea, and a meat pie. Grandma, always 'up' for the underdog bought a couple of dusters from him, and knowing her, probably sent him off with a bit of cake as well. She might even have invited him in out of the cold, and given him a cup of tea. I don't know – I only heard what she told grandad!

But I do know - a few days later, a letter was dropped through the letter box. It had been signed by a number of residents from the houses around us, and stated that on no account are hawkers, beggars, or tramps, tolerated in the avenue, and they suggested grandma had a plaque made to put on the front garden gate to show this.

I don't know what else grandma said, probably a lot! I don't know if she replied to their letter, or ignored them – but I do remember one thing she said! and meant –

'Right! That's it! We're moving!'

In no time at all, boxes were packed, books were stacked, of which grandad had a thousand! Emergency rations were taken out of the larder and carefully sealed and labelled. Nobody could make up a parcel like my grandad. There was string and sealing wax everywhere.

That dark day in winter, we waited all day for the furniture removal men to arrive. With the blackouts taken down, nowhere to sit, nowhere to cook, I had not been in grandad's good books when I'd sat on the best lamp shade, because I couldn't see what it was in the dim light in the hallway, our lives changed again.

Goodbye June! Goodbye Roe Lea School! Goodbye Mr. Chambers! Goodbye Anderson Shelter! Also, alas, it was goodbye to a gleaming white inside bathroom and toilet, a large back garden, a third bedroom, and the quietness of the tree lined avenue. The paid up red rent book was given back to the Town Hall, and a new one acquired from the Co-operative Society, who owned the house we were going to live in, next to their grocery store. A house on the main road, where the trams went noisily by every few minutes, and a railway line faced us, on top of a grassy incline at the other side of the road. Our house was adjoined to another house, the doorsteps only inches apart, a long strip of garden at the front, that later, my grandma made really nice. A steep backyard, with two deep stone steps up to the cold damp outside toilet. Four rooms and a tiny scullery, 'that you couldn't swing a cat in!' grandma remarked.

What possessed them I'll never know, to make such a bad move!

So now we lived at 235 Whalley New Road, where grandma – God love her, made the best of things, for many years, until the day she died there.

How they managed to get all their belongings into that small house, was a miracle. 'A work of art!' said grandma. The front room, for a very long time, stored grandad's one thousand books. The back room was the *living* room. A huge oak sideboard took the space of one wall. On it sat two ornaments, one at either side. A gentleman and his lady. Grandad's grey trilby hat covered the head and shoulders of the gentleman, and grandma's little black astrakhan hat covered the lady, so that only the legs of the figures were ever seen.

Waiting for Aunty Rene to come to play it on a Sunday afternoon stood the heavy iron framed piano, taking up another wall. Under the large sash window, that looked out into the dark yard, (dark, because the co-op storeroom blocked out the light) was a big wooden table, used for everything. Meals were served on it every day. Ironing was done on it on Tuesdays, baking was done on it on Fridays. An easy chair for grandad, a rocking chair for grandma, a stool for me, and a small sofa were arranged around the open fireplace. At grandad's side was the radio, where he could fiddle the knobs to change the programmes. On the fireside wall, by the window, was a massive brown cupboard, holding anything and everything. Over the fire, hanging from the ceiling was a rack, showing all our neatly washed and ironed clothes. But taking pride of place, above all, was a tiny sewing cabinet, that grandma kept her sewing things in. The brass handles on the drawers were lion's heads, with a ring through each of their noses. It was a cherished present from grandad.

A cold flagged floor scullery led off from the living room.

An ugly stone mottled brown slopstone sat under the window, with one cold water tap protruding from its middle. A wash boiler, with a gas jet underneath, and a gas oven, that blew out, because of the gaps around the back door that let in the draughts, made up the picture, with a too small kitchenette to complete it. The rooms of the house divided themselves with a steep dark stairway, leading to the two bedrooms. The front one overlooking the main road, the back one, I shared with Eva, overlooked the back yard, and the backs of the houses beyond. Under the stairs, a cubby hole by the side of the piano, replaced the Anderson shelter. In went torches, books, blankets, flasks – and the bucket! In went grandad, grandma, and me, for the first few nights of moving there; then grandad was called to do firewatching duties at the abattoirs in the town centre. Grandma said Hitler wasn't getting her out of her warm bed anymore, so we never sat under the stairs again. She decided if the worst should happen, we would be safer sitting under the table. At least we would be able to get out if the window was blown in on top of us. When grandad went firewatching, she let me sleep in her big bed. When we had said our prayers, and 'Good night, God bless' she always added – 'We're all in as matters!' I always wanted to ask, 'What about Grandad?' but I never did.

# CHAPTER SIX

Like magic, a house, seemingly without character, was changed into a home. Familiar smells of cooking drifted through the air – neckend stews, oxtail soup, pies, cakes, and grandma's speciality – coconut macaroons. On certain days other aromas took over. The smell of freshly ironed linen on Tuesdays, and on Sundays, 1711 cologne, when grandma put on one of her better dresses, her mother of pearl earrings, and a dab of scent behind each ear.

Miss Warburton was our next door neighbour. A neat, fussy, but friendly little person. Not more than five feet tall, she wore spectacles with lens that magnified her eyes to twice their size. Her black hair was plaited in coils, one round each ear, looking like earphones. I soon invited myself into her house, that was tidy and dark. Photographs of her dead relations, going back to the early 1800s, stared down at me from the walls. Her table was covered with a green velvet cloth, with tassles round the edge. She invited me for tea one day. While I was there, I asked her if I could stay the night, and sleep with her. 'Oh! You had better ask your grandma,' she said. I'm sure she hoped grandma would say no, which she did. I must have insisted, but the answer was still No!

Grandma thought wanting to sleep with Miss Warburton very funny, she laughed and laughed, and on Sunday when Aunt Rene came round, I heard grandma say to her – 'I can't think of anything worse than sleeping with Miss Warburton, but there's no accounting for taste!'

Another new school! Cedar Street Junior School, one minute away from home, was full, due to an influx of evacuees – children from London, and dockland areas, where bombs had been raining down on them every night. These children had left their homes and their parents, and taken by train to safer parts of the country. They assembled in schools and church halls, where people went to view them, to see if they would like to have them to stay in their homes for the duration. Sometimes siblings were split up, as people found it difficult to take two or three children. These tired little souls waited for someone to 'pick them out.' A few days later, they started to attend the nearest school.

Members from the town council called at houses asking if they'd room to take in an evacuee. When they came to grandma's, she had to tell them how many rooms were in the house, and how many people lived in them. Some children were lucky, some were not, as the luck of the draw was made as to who would house them. Letters were found pinned to their vests, sometimes with a £1 note from their mothers, who had no choice but to let them go, in the hope it would save their lives. Pleading letters to an unknown person, saying 'Please, please look after my child'.

Whalley Range School, to me a monster of a building, was quite a walk away, down the hill to Whalley Range. Sliding down the icy hilly streets every morning in winter was something I hated. The stone flagged schoolyard, was situated on an incline, with wide steps leading up to the toilets. Coming down them was treacherous. They were like glass when they were covered in black ice, and still like glass when the snow fell on them. Us little ones came down them by the side of the wall, or on our bottom's, slipping, sliding, and falling.

Whalley Range School hasn't much of a place in my memory. Making a Christmas Card for my grandma, when the boy in the desk behind borrowed my red crayon, and did not giving it back, so that I had to finish Santa's red cloak in pink, stays in my mind, but only because grandma kept that card for forty years before she passed it on to me.

Christmas came again with people making the best of it. We had a chicken for Christmas dinner. Aunt Rene and my cousin Averil came to share it with us. I didn't see Averil very often, so although she was the same age as me, we were not friends. Grandma had managed to get a jar of mincemeat from the Co-op, and made mince tarts. Grandad had bought her a large circular box of chocolate liquors. Tiny bottles made of delicious chocolate, all wrapped in different colours of silver paper, containing some of the most peculiar tasting drinks, like whiskey, rum, gin, cherry brandy, and sherry. I was allowed to have a cherry brandy one, seeing that it was Christmas.

I don't know if Father Christmas came to the evacuees. It troubled me a bit wondering if he knew where they all lived, but grandma said he did.

He knew where I lived that year of 1941.

Waking very early on Christmas morning, I sat up in bed to see a long box at the foot of it. When I took off the lid, there was the most wonderful dolly I had ever seen. I picked her up, and as she turned, she said, 'Mama.' Her bright blue eyes opened and shut. Her pert red lips showed two small white teeth. Her cheeks were rosy, and her hair was ginger. She was dressed in a green velvet hat and coat, that Mrs. Christmas had made, underneath was her silky pink dress, with a pattern of pansies. She wasn't made of celluloid, but of smooth shiny pot.

On the back of her neck was her name – 'Rosebud!' Did real babies come with their names on the back of their neck? I didn't know. I also didn't know that Rosebud would be with me through thick and thin for the rest of my life.

I decided I didn't like going to school. I hadn't made any friends there, and I didn't like boys! My golliwog that I took to school, grandma had knit for me, with his bright red jacket, black bow tie, and white buttons for his eyes, had been ruined by boys! Two of them had taken my golly, and between them, pulled and pulled and pulled him, until they stretched him so much, that when I took him home, hanging over my arm, he was about 6ft long. So I decided school wasn't for me. I pleaded with my grandma that school wasn't necessary. I could read. I could help at home. I'd iron the hankies and all the tea towels. I'd shell the peas when I was asked. I could go errands to the Co-op shop next door. I wouldn't speak when the news was on the radio – but to no avail! 'I'd have the school inspector round in no time,' she said. – She did, many times.

I decided to be ill – every morning at 8.30! I didn't realize what a wonderful actress I was, but sometimes I really did feel sick, and sometimes I really was sick – in the slopstone, with grandma holding my hand. 'She should get an Oscar for this,' I once heard her say, but I didn't know what an Oscar was. So most days I had to go to school.

But life wasn't all doom and gloom – we were going to get a dog! – also – when I was sick in the mornings, I started to go a lovely yellowy colour. So when that happened the doctor was called. After grandma had paid her 3/- for his visit, and chatted to him for a while, I was allowed to stay off school for two whole weeks – to iron my hankies, and shell my peas.

On one of the rare occasions when I was at school, I couldn't get home quick enough the day grandad was bringing the dog home. Why we couldn't have had a little dog, I didn't understand, one I could cuddle or wheel out in my dolly's pram – but no, there was this huge furry orange dog, with a big black tongue. 'It's a Chow,' said grandad, 'and we had to have a big dog, because a little one would get under grandma's feet and she would fall over it. It's called Beauty!'

Beauty by name, but not by nature. I didn't have a lot to do with Beauty. He zoomed through the front door as soon as it was opened, ran down the main road, barking at people, and running after the trams, almost getting himself mangled under the wheels. If taken for a walk, he would squiggle and squirm until he got off the lead, then run like the wind trying to find a pile of manure. That was easy to find, because the milkman and coalman came by horse and cart – he would roll over and over in the manure, until his thick orange coat was covered in it; then, he wouldn't come when he was called! Grandad would come back angry and exhausted. He took Beauty straight into the backyard to clean him before grandma would let him in the house.

One day Beauty went – just went! 'He's gone to live somewhere else,' said grandma. So that was that!

Each morning the atmosphere in the house was tense. Grandma waited anxiously for the postman. She made numerous trips to the front door to see if he had dropped the letters through the letterbox without her hearing him. If he didn't call, she consoled herself and us, by saying, 'Well, no news is good news,' It was news from Burma she waited for, from 'Little Frank.'

About every three weeks a parcel arrived. Battered and

torn, these parcels made there way by boat and train, from the heat of the jungle, all the way to Whalley New Road. As soon as she got it into her hands, grandma took it through the house, and into the backyard. Between them, her and grandad scrutinised the writing, the stamps, the postmarks, before grandad cut the string and pulled the wrapping paper apart; then with the aid of fire tongs, he lifted the contents out, one by one, and laid them on the ground. The smell was awful! 'Keep away!' grandad told me, 'these could have insects on them that bite!' So I kept away!

But grandma picked them up as soon as she could, and fondled them with tears in her eyes, and love in her heart. 'Little Frank's socks!' she said. 'My poor little Frank!'

Little Frank's socks! About ten pairs of them, muddy and steaming! No letter was enclosed, that wasn't allowed. Only the 'Red Cross' address of where they had come from. For the next week, grandma busied herself lovingly washing and darning the socks, when grandad would pack them up again carefully, along with another two or three pairs, that grandma had knitted. Bars of chocolate, cigarettes, and long letters, including one from me, were added, ready to be taken to the G.P.O on Darwen St; and sent on their long journey back to the jungle.

I do not remember anyone taking me to school in a morning, or meeting me to take me home in the afternoon. It took me a long time to walk home from school. I either took different routes to avoid boys I didn't like, or dogs that barked at me, or to pass shop windows I wanted to look in.

A surprise awaited me one afternoon when I eventually reached home. Parked outside of the front door was a baby's pram. When I walked in the house, there was a lady sitting in grandad's chair, with a baby on her knee. 'This is your mother,' said grandma, 'and this is your baby sister.' I don't think I'd remembered my mother, but I was pleased she came, because she'd brought me some patent black shoes, wrapped in soft tissue paper, in a white box. They were far too big, because she hadn't known my size, but I looked at them every day for months until my feet grew into them.

If the war was making any difference to my life, and it must have been, I was not to notice. I soon got used to having no fruit, one egg a week, and no sugar in my tea.

A big bin was put on the corner of each street. P.S painted on, in large letters. It meant 'pig swill.' All the left over food from the families in each house in the street had to be put in the bins. They were then taken away, and the food fed to farm animals. Our garden gate and railing was taken away for ammunitions – to make bullets and bombs to fight Hitler with. But, these things didn't make a lot of difference to me. I still sat on the doorstep, reading my 'Chick's Own' or 'Sunny Stories,' that I'd now progressed to, or nursing Rosebud. I knew the times when the trains went by, across the road, on top of the grassy incline, and would sit and wait for them, and wave to the driver and the fireman as they went past. They got to know me, and would wave back.

One day my grandma managed to get some cherries. I thought they were lovely things, beautiful deep shiny red, far too nice to eat, especially the double ones. So I put them over my ears, and sat on the doorstep waiting for the trains to pass. I put my hair, still short and straight, behind my ears, to show off my cherries to the train drivers. 'I've never known anybody like you,' said my grandma.

Grandad checked and rechecked the blackouts on the windows, as well as the batteries for our torches. I hated the shadowy darkness I saw if I peeped through the bedroom window at night. No lamps lit the streets. Inside the house was not much lighter. A gas mantle, hanging from the ceiling in the middle of the room, supplied us with a poor light. Two delicate chains on either side of the mantle, controlled the flow of gas. To light it, grandma pulled the chain on the left hand side, and held a lit taper to the mantle. It lit with a 'pop;' then she gently pulled the chain down to increase the flow of gas, and the amount of light grandad told her was adequate for the room. We always had more light when he was out!

If the mantle broke, as it did often, because they were as delicate as spider's webs, it produced an irritating pop popping noise, and a blue flame blew out from it.

We'd settled at 235, as it was to be called from then on. Grandad continued his job as a clerk, and dutifully did his firewatching bit. Aunt Eva worked in the gown shop, although clothing coupons had been issued, and buying clothes was limited. If a girl was getting married, people would pool their clothing coupons to buy the bride's dress – if she was lucky enough to get one! Women became thrifty, although they always had been in Lancashire. Most clothes were made at home. Winter coats could be made out of thick 'army blankets, 'a regulation grey, but cleverly made to look fashionable, if a strip of coloured material was stitched around the hem! Bloomers and blouses could be made out of parachute material, soft, grey and silky, that servicemen nicked by the yard for their women folk back home.

Eva and me still sang at night in our beds. Miss Warburton next door loved hearing us through the bedroom wall. Her and grandma were now very friendly. They chatted together in the spring evenings as they stood on their doorsteps – but of course, they didn't neighbour! Grandma was happier at 235, she said. She enjoyed her visits to Blackburn Market on Wednesdays, and Saturdays when I went with her. A wonderful market! After she'd shopped for knitting wool, bits of material, and any fruit and vegetables that were available, we had a glass of homebrewed sarsaparilla, or a small dish of mushy peas, sprinkled with mint sauce. We bought a large bag of broken biscuits from a stall in the market hall, where a young boy with bright ginger hair, served us – 'What a lovely lad!' said grandma. I didn't think much of him myself, but little did I know I was going to meet him again, when I was seventeen, a student nurse, and that he was going to take me to see that great epic film - Gone With The Wind!

After buying oat cakes for our tea and black puddings for Sunday breakfast next day, we went home on the tram. I liked Saturday afternoons with my grandma!

We didn't go out visiting very often. People stayed in at night. The cinema, called 'The Star Cinema' not far from us, opened every week night. The main interest was the showing of the newsreel, when folks could see how the war was progressing. The films were light hearted, with Bob Hope and Bing Crosby. Glamour was introduced into my life, when I was first allowed to go, to see Betty Grable, and Dorothy Lamour in her lovely sarong. Children were not allowed to watch the newsreels, and we had to stand out in the foyer. I was crazy about the cinema. It switched me on to a new world. I would go at every given opportunity. It finished at 9.30 p.m, so I was allowed to go with grandad, sometimes on Fridays, if he wasn't firewatching.

If I couldn't go to the cinema, I would go with grandma to

visit two of her friends. Polly and Maggie were sisters, who grandma had known since they were in the girl guides together at St. Michael's Church when they were very young. They didn't live far away, but to get to their house, we had to walk under the railway bridge. In the blackout it was pitch black! I took a book to read, while they swapped gossip; then there was always something nice to eat. Either a cake that grandma had taken, or something special that they had prepared, just for us. We always left early, and they would shout 'Bye Bye! Bye Bye!' until we got to the railway bridge. As we passed underneath, grandma would hold my arm tight, and start a conversation with me – 'Polly looked well tonight, didn't she Tom?' or 'Did you pick up your scarf Tom?' She would squeeze my arm, and that would mean I hadn't to answer. She went on like this until we had passed under the bridge. I thought it very funny, but never knew how frightened she was for both of us, as we walked together in those dark streets.

Polly and Maggie didn't visit us. They were getting older, and would stay at home, apart from a visit to their corner shop. Grandma's relatives came when they could, her sisters, Miriam, Maggie, and Eva, and her brothers – George, Alan, and Henry. Now and then, her father came. Jonathon Whiteside was a sprightly old man, in his nineties, and as sharp as a needle. Small and wiry, he came up the garden path with the aid of two walking sticks. Over numerous cups of tea, he reminisced, keeping me highly amused. My favourite story he told was about the time he was a fruit merchant. He delivered the fruit on his cart, drawn by his lovely horse, named Dolly. When he'd finished his rounds, he would go into his local pub for a well earned pint of ale – and Dolly would continue home by herself, pulling the cart behind her!

He came from Knott End, where my grandma was born. When his family increased, he and his wife Eva Elizabeth, (nee - Wolfe Singleton) decided to move to Lancashire to be sure of work in the cotton industry. Sadly, one of his daughters, Ivy, drowned herself in the canal. None of the family ever spoke of this. I think it could have been because she lost her sweetheart in the first world war. I loved great grandad coming to see us. He was a wonderful story teller.

Reluctantly I went to school, in between the times I turned yellow, when I was promptly kept at home, to my delight.

It was during one of these times that I watched my grandma making a huge cake. It was baked in a special tin, borrowed from the Co-op's confectionary department. Aunt Rene came to help, putting white icing on the top with ribbons and tiny silver balls. It was very special, grandma told me. Uncle Frank had been posted back to England for a while, and he was coming home on leave. I went ecstatic! My Uncle Frank was coming back! He could take me out again! We were going to have a party! Grandma had made him a cake! 'Is it his birthday?' I asked. 'No,' grandma said, 'He's got married! And he's bringing his new wife home to meet us, before he goes back to Burma!'

# CHAPTER SEVEN

Rejection must be the strongest hurt above all other.

If certificates were given for handling it, I'd have been given one with honours later in my life.

The day my Uncle Frank brought his new wife Alice home, was my first hurtful experience, the very first in a long line of many.

The wedding cake took pride of place on the table. Grandad got a day off work, and put on his best grey suit, with his watch and chain. When everything in the kitchen was prepared, grandma changed into one of her best dresses. She kept two for special occasions, a maroon, and a grey one. Aunt Eva and Rene were there – and then Frank came – with Alice!

There was great kissing and hugging and Congratulations. She was much taller than him, and very well built. She had a pretty face, and a lovely smile, showing perfect white teeth. Her blue W.A.A.F uniform suited her well. Her face was framed with a shock of dark ginger curly hair. She came from Lincoln, so didn't speak like us, but with an attractive 'twangy' accent.

After I'd had a good look at her, I took my stool, and went to sit at the other side of the piano where nobody could see me. Sherry was poured into tiny glasses, and sandwiches handed round. Alice and Frank cut the cake, and the others clapped their hands. Nobody missed me – until Aunt Rene cut the cake into slices, and handed it round. 'Where's our Pip?'

she asked. (Pip was always her pet name for me.) I stayed where I was! She popped her head round the piano. I had to come out. So I ate my cake; then went into the front room, to sit on my own among my grandad's books. Some time later, what seemed like days to me, grandma came in. Why was I being so surly? I tried to explain. I was going to marry Frank! My grandma had a little talk to me. She was kind, but must have been very tongue in cheek, when she put an arm round me and said – 'No! It is not because you have lost your front teeth, and it isn't because you haven't got curly hair. It's because you are only seven and not allowed to marry your Uncle Frank!

The independent streak that I was born with was allowed to develop. Not only did I take myself to and from school, but now I went to the shops on my own.

The Post Office at Bastwell, an area about a mile from our house, at the crossroad between Whalley New Road and Whalley Range, was where I like to go on my own. On Saturday mornings I went to buy a sixpenny saving stamp to stick in my National Saving Stamp Book, and to look at all the lovely things in the shop, especially at Christmas time, when at the back of the shop was a fairy grotto, with tiny flickering lights. There was a Christmas tree with baubles, that reflected the presents and toys on the shelves. I didn't know just how depleted those shelves were, or how wonderful the shop was before the war. People made what they could of what they had, and I thought it was one of the nicest shops ever. I spent a long time inside, before I continued to the wool shop next door. All kinds of coloured knitting wool filled the window, among knitting patterns of socks, balaclava helmets, mittens, and my most favourite of all – a pattern of a baby's white shawl, with a picture of a beautiful black shiny 'silver cross' pram. The feathery white shawl was draped across the pram. The pram hood was up, so I couldn't see the baby inside. A nurse stood by the pram, resplendent in her uniform, wearing a nurse's cap – a crisp white triangle that wrapped round her head, and fastened at the back of her neck. I stared and stared at the lovely picture – and decided – when I grew up I would be a nurse, and look like her!

Things were happening! Grandad took me on my first train ride from Blackburn to Darwen, the next town, a few miles away. The vastness and darkness of Blackburn Railway Station was daunting. I held my grandad's hand tight, and even tighter as the great steam train rattled towards us, screeching so loud as it braked, that I clapped my hands over my ears. Most of the journey was through a long tunnel. The anticipation of it all, and going, as I thought, at the speed of lightening, nearly made me sick, but when I recovered, I wanted to go again.

I'd now joined Blackburn Public Library. Grandad was a regular visitor there, and left me in the junior section to choose three books, while he lost himself in philosophy, great statesmen, and politics, forgetting all about time, and sometimes forgetting all about me. If he wasn't ready to go when I was, I would walk up the great stairway too the top of the library building. Stuffed animals with beady eyes sat in glass cases for all time, and huge pictures of old people who had been good citizens of Blackburn, surrounded me.

If I still could not drag grandad away, I wandered out of the library, and onto Ainsworth Street, near to the Town Hall. There, was another museum, with a lovely bow window. I

looked through at the tall spinning wheel inside. Written on a
shiny plague was 'Arkwright's Spinning Jenny.' A model of
Mr. Arkwright, made out of wax, stood at the wheel. Baskets
of raw cotton surrounded him. Another wax model of a lady
in a long dress, with a lace pinny over, stood in a corner. She
wore a frilly cap on her head. I suppose it was Mrs. Arkwright.
The scene in this window never changed. I knew it in detail, as
I gazed at it so many times in my childhood, during the good
and the bad times.

The grown ups had their worries, and I had mine.
The biggest one at that time was a brown wire haired
mongrel dog, called Peter. He'd come to live further down the
road, and like Beauty, he got out of the house where he lived,
and ran after the trams that passed by. Not only that, he ran
after people, jumping up at them, - and – he ran after me!
Because of him, I hated the name Peter, until I grew up, fell in
love, and married someone with that name! But then, I was
terrified of that silly dog. Grandma had to go to the front
door to see if he was about, before I would venture out. She'd
say, 'No, Peter's not about. You can come out!' But as I
walked a few yards down the road, he would come springing
out from somewhere, and make right for me. If I ran, he ran
after me, and barked and barked.
Like Beauty, one day he disappeared! I never saw him
again!

Peter the dog was quickly replaced by another fear. A boy
called 'Monkey Face' was after me. I suppose it was because I
shouted Monkey Face at him, if I thought I was at a safe
distance. He too ran after me. One day he caught me! I ran up
somebody's garden path at the time, and shouted to him that I

lived there, that we had moved. But he knew where I lived. There was no escape, and he kept me there till I said I was sorry!

Good News! Mrs Eatough was coming back into my life. 'She's coming to see you on Sunday,' said grandma. The thought of Mrs Eatough coming to see me conjured up thoughts of sweets, cakes and lucky bags. I couldn't wait for Sunday!

At ten minutes to two, the letter box sounded its familiar rap, and there was my lovely Mrs Eatough, wearing a flowery hat. 'Hello! Little Joyce,' she said, 'Are you ready?'

'Yes, she's ready,' said grandma. Turning to me, she told me, 'Mrs Eatough's taking you to Sunday School at Hawthorn Street Methodist Church.'

Oh! No! How could they? Sunday School? School on a Sunday? I pleaded my usual plea. 'I can't go, Aunt Rene's coming!'

'She'll be here when you get back. Now put your hat and coat on,' said grandma. They didn't believe me when I said I felt sick, and off I had to go.

'You'll love it,' said Mrs Eatough, as we walked along Whalley New Road into Hawthorn Street. I knew I wouldn't, and I didn't!

She hadn't brought me any sweets either!

Once inside the church, I was directed to a classroom at the side of the big hall. I sat at a table with other children I did not know. I was given a picture of Jesus to crayon, with crayons to be shared, which I hated.

We had to be quiet, as a man was speaking in the hall; then people sang hymns to an organ that was played in the corner. When we had finished crayoning our pictures of Jesus, we put our hands together and sang – 'Thank you for the world so sweet.' We filed into the hall, among the grown ups. I sat on a long wooden form, next to Mrs Eatough, while a man at a big desk told me how bad I'd been, (along with all the others,) - that I hadn't! What a sinner I was – that I wasn't! How I should believe in Jesus – that I couldn't and wouldn't!

I tried all ways to get out of going to Sunday School, and some of the time, succeeded. I must have gone quite a few Sundays though, because at Christmas, I got a prize – a religious book – 'Little Lamb Who Made Thee.'

The promise of going to Entwhistle's Ice Cream Shop, after Sunday School, must have kept me going through that long hour of endurance. Entwhistles was a large wooden hut on Cedar Street. Inside were vast machines that made delicious ice cream. Even during the war, we still had ice cream, thank goodness! People crowded in there on Sunday afternoons, to see the choc' ices being made. Small blocks of white ice cream were placed on a machine that lifted them into the air; then, gently dipped them into a huge vat of thick chocolate. It lifted them out again, the chocolate dripping from them, as they were placed on a tray to set. When set, another machine skilfully wrapped each one in soft blue and white paper, with Entwhistles written all over it!

The war dragged on! I didn't see what all the fuss was about, and decided when I grew up I would sort it out and make everybody happy again. I would get a gun, and go to Germany, wherever that was, and shoot Hitler – point blank! I'd seen it done on the films, and it looked dead easy.

Meantime – grandma was over the moon, because they'd got some lemons at the Co-op shop, next door, and she'd managed to get three! She brought them out of her basket, and placed them on the table. 'Pancakes and homemade lemonade,' she declared. Thinking they were like oranges, but a different colour, I asked if I could have one. I was told I wouldn't like them, and they were only for cooking with. Next time grandma went to the shops, I decided I would try one. Of course I would like them! I cut a lemon in half, and took a mouthful! I realized I'd made a mistake. She would be cross. I wrote her a note, in red crayon, on a large sheet of paper – 'Dear Grandma. I don't like lemons after all!' I stuck it on the front door, where she couldn't miss it! She came in with my note in her hand. 'You know what's wrong with you Joyce? Your eyes are greedier than your belly!' I kept silent. She rescued the lemon, and nothing more was said. She reminded me of it years later, when I visited her with children of my own.

Uncle Frank went back to Burma. He didn't send his socks home to be washed anymore. Not only had I lost him, but grandma had lost him as well, as so often happens with sons.

I don't remember Alice visiting us when she left the W.A.A.F.S to have her baby, neither did my mother come to see us, or my dad.

My mother had left her family in Florence Street, and got a house of her own in Hodson Street, a street with terraced houses at the bottom end of Whalley Range, near to the town centre. Alice lived a few streets away from her. I heard grandma say 'Those two are as thick as thieves!' Apparently, I had two sisters now. Although I never heard my grandma ever say a wrong word about my mother, I sensed there was ill feeling between them.

We had no photographs of 'royalty' in the house. Grandad cut articles and photos out of the newspapers, but never of the royals. I heard about the two little princesses, one way or another. How beautiful, well behaved, and good at everything they were. Pictures of the King and Queen were shown on the newsreels at the Star Cinema, as they walked around the bombed sites in London. Grandma said to grandad, 'Anyone walking among people who had just lost their homes and families, dressed in fur and wearing pearls, should be locked up!' Grandma also said Churchill was a 'war monger!'

I listened in – as we sat round the fire at night, during the winters of their discontent. Grandma pointed out pictures in the fire. 'Look! There's a man's face! See his beard?' She pointed to mystical shapes with the long poker that stood on the fender.

She taught me to knit with large wooden needles. The stitches would drop, and the whole thing become so tight in my hot sticky hands, that she would have to take it over from me to sort out, so I could start again.

We made hankies from scraps of material, bought in bundles, from the local mills. She taught me to stitch a shell edging; then when I became reasonably good, I was allowed to do it on my underslips.

Now and then grandad would look up from his newspaper to read out snippets, or give his view on things I could not understand. Sometimes he would decide to test me on my adding up. Arithmetic was not my strong point. I could never remember my multiplication tables, they just wouldn't stick in my head, although all the songs I learned from the films stayed in. '7+4? 6+5? 5+9?' grandad would ask. Grandma who was quietly knitting, would hold up her fingers to supply me with the answer. When she didn't want to listen to his theories on life, she pretended she was counting her stitches on her knitting needle. When she had no choice but to endure his religious and political reasonings, she said nothing, just nodded. When he stopped talking, to listen to the news, and for grandma to make the cocoa, she folded up her knitting, placed it on the arm of her chair, stood up, smoothed down her pinny, and walking into the kitchen, would say softly, having the last word – 'Well, somebody puts the colours in the flowers!'

She was smart, my grandma! So much cleverer than anyone ever gave her credit for!

My new Auntie Alice, brought her new baby Pauline, in her new big black shiny 'silver cross' pram, just like the one in the knitting pattern picture in the shop window at Bastwell. I was in raptures! The long school holidays lay ahead, and Pauline was to come every day, while Alice went to work at the local factory. I didn't care if we hadn't room for a big pram, or a baby, or if it was all too much for my grandma. I was going to love it.

I was allowed to take Pauline out in her pram, all the way along the road, if I promised not to cross the main road. She was a lovely baby, with a soft blonde curl on top of her head. Everyone stopped to speak to her, and to tell me how good I was for taking such care of her. I sat her up; then laid her down, sat her up; then laid her down again and again and again. But I did take care of her. At home, I was allowed to have drinks of her ministry supplied orange juice, and spoonfuls of her Virol, and Rose Hip Syrup – everything was rosy, until, one day, my grandma said to me –'You have got to start visiting your mother. She wants you to go down there on Saturdays – starting this week!'

## CHAPTER EIGHT

Pleading time again! 'I can't go to my mothers, I don't know where she lives, and anyway, I go to the library on Saturday mornings, and I go to the market on Saturday afternoons – So I can't!'

Grandma could see in into the future, and what this was all going to lead to. She could see it would start with visits to my mother that would last longer and longer, until one day the visit would last for good. She looked at me thoughtfully. Stroking my hair, she said, 'I think you'd better go love. We don't want any trouble!'

Dressed in my best green coat, with its velvet collar, and a satin ribbon in my hair, I walked down Whalley New Road, past my favourite knitting shop at Bastwell, and onto Whalley Range. I knew I had to walk to the very end, almost into the town. In my pocket was a piece of paper with 41, Hodson Street, written on it.

My memory has blanked out that first visit to my mother's house. I remember vaguely two younger children being there, but I can't remember what was said to me, or what I did. I remember asking, 'Can I go now?' at the end of the day, when dusk was descending. I walked the long walk back to my grandma, who was standing on the doorstep waiting for me, as the sky got darker. I'd missed my visit to the library, and grandma had been to the market without me, and that's how it was going to be from then on.

Mrs Eatough had given up on me. On Sunday afternoons

I was allowed to stay at home, and sit upstairs with my grandma. Her legs were now quite bad. Although she must have been only in her late forties, the phlebitis was worsening. Instead of walking out on Sunday, she put a chair by the window in her front bedroom, and looked out at the people passing by. Cars were few. People walked to the cemetery or to the parks. She had a wicked sense of humour, and remarked on the people as they passed. 'Oh! Dearie me! Look at that hat! I'd have stayed in rather than have worn that on my head.' – or– 'Look at these two coming along! Well, I must say they don't spoil another couple!' Her comments, not always unkind, made us laugh together, until it was time for me to go to Entwhistle's for the choc' ices.

On the Sunday my Aunt Rene brought my cousin Averil, things went wrong. She sat upstairs with us, and happened to kick my grandma's bad leg, accidentally or not, I don't know. Grandma was in great pain. I must have thought it wasn't an accident, and I'm afraid I dragged Averil to the top of the stairs, and threw her down. There was a bit of a rumpus between the adults. I never saw much of Averil after that.

My grandparents were buzzing! Uncle Frank's regiment was going to be shown on the films at the Majestic Cinema. Every night for a week, the boys from home would come on the screen, with a message for their loved ones. All the way from Burma!

The lights in the cinema dimmed. The film started with music, while the camera zoomed into the jungle. In turn, the men came close up on the screen, each giving their message. Then came my lovely Uncle Frank. There he was, looking hot in an open neck khaki short sleeved shirt, and matching shorts, with a huge hat, tipped up at one side. He was self conscious, having to talk to us on camera. He smiled – and said, 'Hello Mum and Dad, and everyone. I hope you are all Ok. Things aren't so bad here. I think of you all, and hope to be back home soon.' Then he smiled again, and said, 'Hello! Little blue eyes!' and gave a well known wink, before they faded him out of the film. It broke my gran's heart to see him – and mine.

'Did you hear the message he sent for me? Did you see him wink at me?' I asked the others, later. 'That was for Pauline,' said Alice. 'Not for you!' But I still thought it was for me.

Very soon after, baby Pauline stopped coming to be minded. I think it was too much for grandma, and grandad 'put his foot down.'

There was much more room in the house again.

In the hallway, by the vestibule door, stood a large mirror. So large, it took up most of the wall. It was there when we moved into the house. So heavy – nobody wanted to move it – and so it stayed. It was covered by an old curtain. When baby Pauline came, the curtain had been removed, so that she could sit in her pram, and look at the other baby looking back at her. It had kept her amused for hours. Now it was keeping me amused, as I preened and pranced in front of it, and acted out the scenes I saw on the films at the Star Cinema, which I frequented regularly now. I sang 'Can't Help Singing' at the top of my voice, pretending I was Deanna Durbin, until grandma had to shut the living room door on me. I saved my red Smarties to smear on my lips, and purted and pouted like Dorothy Lamour. I used all kinds of pretty materials I could lay my hands on, to drape over my head, or hang round my shoulders. My Auntie Eva gave me a pale blue satin dress, with lace coffee coloured short sleeves that I wore continuously. I even took myself into Blackburn, on the tramcar, to a photographer's shop in Church Street, to vainly have my photo taken in it.

When I dressed up, in remnants from my dressing up box, I would ask my grandma – 'Am I nice in this?' Her answer was always the same, 'You're as nice as anyone else! But no nicer!'

Another saying that stayed with me through life!

My ears wafted even more, when I became aware that the adult conversations I listened in to were about me! At grandma's, I overheard – 'She's becoming useful. That's why they want her back! They haven't wanted her up to now! We'll sort it out when our Tom comes back after the war.'

On Saturdays, I heard my mother and Alice talking, - 'Why shouldn't she be at home where she belongs? It's time she was helping out with the others! They only want her there then they don't have to take in an evacuee!'

At my mother's I was asked, 'Who do you want to live with? Your mother or your grandma?'

My mother and Alice together were two imposing characters. I always said, ' I don't know!' 'Well! You are going to have to know!' said my mother.

In between time, I blotted out the cloud that hung over me, and enjoyed the things I liked doing best. I still sat with Rosebud on the doorstep, reading my favourite books, shelling peas, eating Smarties, and waving to the train drivers.

# CHAPTER NINE

My grandparents looked back at the houses they had lived in, and remembered them, fondly or not, by the number of the house. Florence Street was always known as 41. Haston Lea Avenue as 4, and Whalley New Rd; as 235.

Every now and then, on a Sunday, grandad would take me to see his elderly parents, who lived at 21 Accrington Rd. This of course, was 21!

My grandma would say, as we were ready to go, 'Give them my love at 21', or, 'Don't forget to take these cakes I've made for 21.'

We set off in the early afternoon, to walk to the other side of town, first crossing the Wreck. The Wreck was an open space, allocated as a children's play area, with swings, a heavy iron roundabout, and a couple of see- saws. A place I did not like, as grandad had once pushed me so high on a swing, that I came flying off, cutting my knee badly, leaving a white scar that would remind me of the pain for the rest of my life. From the Wreck, we walked up Harwood St. A street shadowed by tall warehouses and factories. One of them a factory where a lot of women in the town worked, making potato crisps. The lovely smell of the cooking crisps permeated the buildings around, as well as seeping into the Wesleyan Chapel, where grandma had once married Herbert!

Halfway up Harwood St, grandad always stopped to pop in to the gent's urinal! These were places for men to 'relieve themselves.' Encased behind a high screen of corrugated iron, painted dark green, they stood dotted about the streets. 'They should take the damn things away, and use them for ammunition,' said grandma.

When grandad went in there, I was so ashamed I walked on. He seemed to take forever, and I agreed with grandma!

Eventually we came to Accrington Rd, a steep road leading from the center of Blackburn to Accrington, the next town on the map. Lined with terraced houses and shops, it was an interesting, busy road, where the trams rode noisily up and down. Number 21 was a toffee shop! Nothing like Mrs Eatough's! There was nothing in the window! A half curtain, made from a piece of faded brown cotton material, hung across, blocking the view inside A tall wooden door, in need of a lick of paint, opened into the barest shop I'd ever seen. The flag floor held a heavy wooden counter that I was allowed to sit on. The shelves behind stocked only a few glass jars of uninteresting sweets. Sarsaparilla drops, Barley Sugar, and mints. Now and then a customer came in, and grandad's father would serve them. A very old gentleman, fairly big, with a thick white moustache, he let me dip my hand in the jar he'd been serving the sweets from, and take one, before he replaced the lid.

The living quarters at the back of the shop were so dark. I can't remember what was in them. Sixteen steps led down from the back door into the yard below. Four communal toilets were built in a row, for use by the residents living in the buildings round them. I always tried not to go!

Coming home from 21, grandad would perform his 'magic tricks'! He came out with 'magic words 'that he made up; then produce sticks of spanish, and sherbet dips from his pocket. I enjoyed this bit! I'd never seen spanish displayed in the shop. I suppose it was kept under the counter, like a lot of things in those days!

I only remember my grandad's mother when she was dying, on one of my last visits to 21. A bed stood in a corner of the dark Victorian living room. Somewhere in it, was a very small, frail old lady. Apart from the odd glance at her, I was not allowed to go near the bed. I stayed in the shop, playing a game of pretending to serve customers.

On the day she died, I do know we stayed a very long time, while grandad filled and refilled hot water bottles to place in her bed.

A few months later, her husband followed her – and for everyone, that was the end of 21!

With the 'war allowance' being allocated to wives of men in the services who had small children, meant they could be exempt from working in the mills, or in the factories on ammunitions. My mother, for the time being, did not go to work, and escaped for once in her life, the early morning treck to spend her day in the noisy weaving sheds. The women in the same position as her, although liberated, took their freedom badly. They missed the companionship, and hated the isolation of 'staying at home.' They spent a lot of their day in each others houses, brewing numerous pots of tea, smoking, washing and setting each others hair, and talking about the other neighbours. Like their mothers before them, they were always on hand for childminding. Borrowing or lending a shilling or two until pay day, and of course, stoning the front step and windowsill on Friday, for any woman in the street who was heavily pregnant.

Reluctantly, I went down to my mothers in Hodson Street on Saturdays.

Perhaps some of the time I enjoyed looking after my younger sisters, especially the baby. My mother never held me, or said anything loving to me. I would have remembered. Then, and all my life, I would remember anything loving and warm that was said to me. I never expected it, and apart from my grandma, very few would pour affection on me, and mean it.

Mr. Jones, the owner of the grocer's shop at the top of Hodson Street, came to know me well – and so he should have! My mother would send me to his shop continuously. As soon as I got back from the shop with one thing, she would send me for another. Again and again my tired young legs walked up Hodson street, and into Mr Jones's 'selling out' shop. Even he would comment – 'Not again, little un! Are you on a route march or summat?' She would send me to the shop when it was getting late, and I wanted to go home to my grandma. "Just go to Jones's before you go,' she'd say. Even though I flew up the street like the wind, hoping the darkness wouldn't come before I was allowed to go - it nearly always did.

At last, I walked back home in the blackout. Sometimes grandad would come to meet me with his torchlight. If not, I would run all the way, knowing my grandma would be standing at her front door waiting for me. In the dark I would hear her shouting my name from a long way off – 'Joyce? Joyce?' When I heard her in the distance, I would run quicker, shouting – 'I'm coming, grandma! I'm nearly home! Grandma? Grandma?'

Out of breath, I would fall into her arms. She knew I hated the severe darkness of the blacked out streets. 'It shouldn't be allowed to happen,' she told my grandad. 'A child of that age should not be out at night anyway. I'm going to write and tell our Tom about it.' Whether she did, I do not know, but nothing altered. In fact, it went worse!

Not often, but once or twice during that year, my mother told me, 'Tell your grandma you are staying the night next week!' I knew better than to protest. Neither did my grandma retaliate. She just shook her head, and packed my toothbrush and nightdress, with no comment.

It was on one of these occasions, just after teatime, my mother told me I was going to look after my baby sisters while she went out. When she told me, I didn't mind so much, because the two new friends I'd made, who lived a few doors higher up the street were to be allowed to stay with me in the house until 8pm. My middle sister was put to bed upstairs, and the baby placed in a small cot by the fireplace downstairs.

My new friends were sisters, a little older than me. I enjoyed going into their house. Their mother was kind and domesticated. Their house was cosy and comfortable.

My mother went out! Where, I did not know. The blackouts had been pulled down on the windows, and with my friends, I looked after the baby, tucking her in, and looking over her. At 8pm, I begged them not to go. I hated the thought of being alone, and the responsibility thrust upon me. Half an hour later their mother came to the house. She was cross with them because they hadn't gone home on time, when told. When she saw me in charge of two small infants – all hell broke loose! She collected us all, and took us back to her house. She informed the other neighbours. When my mother returned, whatever the time, they were waiting for her. There was a great row in the street. My mother carted us all back home, shouting – 'people should mind their own business'. My friend's mother shouted back that she would go to the Town Hall on Monday and report my mother to the cruelty inspector – and she did!

My mind has always been good at blocking out nasty instances in my life. That must have been one of them. What my mother said to me, I don't know!

I didn't go down to her house for some time after that. I did not see my two new friends again!

I knew as much as any small girl should about the war, even a little bit more. Listening to grandad relate the facts of it all to anyone who would listen, watching war films at the Star Cinema, reading my grandma's magazines, with recipes on how to make the most of dried egg, spam and potatoes, and hints, not only how to survive in a bomb blast, but how to tan your legs with gravy browning, which was much more interesting, kept me as informed as I wanted to be.

Two ounces of butter, one egg and a choice at the Co-op, of sugar or jam every week, was no problem to me. Grandma, being a good cook, fed us fairly well, yet we did lack vitamins.

A lot of children suffered from scurvy round their mouths, due to a lack of vitamins, the main one being vitamin C, through not eating enough fruit. I was one of them! The chemist supplied little round cakes of ointment, called 'Snowfire' for this complaint. I had to smear the green gungy stuff round my lips before I went out in the wind or cold, and again at night. It felt like it was burning my lips off, and stung painfully, and didn't do much good.

I knew food was scarce, because every one told you so. At school, at home, in the shops. 'Waste not – want not!' must have been the slogan of all time. Every few weeks we got a banana from the local fruit shop. One for each family, was the rule, but only if they shopped there regularly. Grandma sliced it, and put it in a lemon jelly, that she'd been saving in her stock of special foods at the back of the kitchenette; then we all had some of it for Sunday tea. Auntie Eva bought Blackcurrant Puree from the pharmacy, when she could get it. It was expensive, but she let me have a big spoonful every morning.

Life went on. By now I'd had my eighth birthday. I thought birthday parties were things that happened to other people, or to girls like Shirley Temple, or the two princesses, Elizabeth and Margaret Rose. I didn't expect one, had never had one, and would never have one! Another hard winter had gone by. Sometimes the heat was on at school, sometimes not, depending on how much coke was delivered to keep their boilers running. When the classrooms became unbearable, we were sent home. It was always warm in my grandma's house. She made sure we got our supply of coal. When the coalman came with his horse and cart every month, she would wait for him. Before he humped the sacks of coal or coke into the back yard, dropping them in the corner, she came out with a pot of tea for him; then went behind the lace curtain at the kitchen window, to count the sacks as he brought them in. When he'd finished, she would ask if he could spare an extra sack. If he did, she gave him a small glass of sherry!

'It's not bribery,' she would say, later. 'It's 'need must the devil drives, or God helps them who helps themselves!'

The thought of the long school holidays in the summer seemed my only reason to go to school. I'd been to the school clinic on Victoria Street, and queued in the lines with other children to have my sniff of gas, while some of my teeth were removed. I wasn't ever taken to the dentist. It was something I endured all by myself. One time after a visit there, I sat on the stone steps outside of the clinic for ages, waiting for my head to clear, spitting blood out onto the pavement.

The school doctor had spent days at our school. We were weighed and examined. Standing in our vests and knickers, we waited to go behind the screen to see the doctor, one by one. The girls went first, laughing and giggling to hide our nervousness. I was seen by the doctor twice because I kept turning yellow. He was concerned.

Blackburn had still escaped the bombing. It was peaceful. Grandad did his firewatching. Grandma planted wallflowers, lupins and pansies in the front garden. Miss Warburton did the same in hers! Uncle Frank had been posted back to England, because he had malaria. To me, life was normal!

Films and film stars were playing a big part in my life. Laurel and Hardy and Charlie Chaplin made me laugh. Sometimes I laughed because everyone else in the cinema laughed. The Three Stooges, I thought were stupid! Shirley Temple showed off too much. Donald Duck – I couldn't tell what he said! Dorothy Lamour and Paulette Goddard were lovely, and Betty Grable was 'common'. My grandma said so! Tyrone Power looked a bit like my dad, if I could remember what my dad looked like!

It was through the cinema I learned people had better homes, better schools, and spoke better than we did. The American influence showed me a life that was lived in a land that was always sunny, where people sang songs all the time, under palm trees, next to a blue sea, just like I'd seen it in books. I realized from watching the films, that when I grew up, I could buy clothes from shops, and not still have the ones grandma made for me then.

I imagined myself grown up. Common or not, like Betty Grable I would have a big white Cadillac, and dress in white fur. I would ride in the white Cadillac down Hodson Street, to see my mother on Saturday afternoons. All the neighbours would come out to see me!

My realms of fantasy would always be a form of escapism, but were to be squashed sooner than I knew!

My mother moved from Hodson Street, to Freme Street. Another street of terraced houses, where the river Blakewater ran along the bottom. She now lived two streets away from Alice, and not quite as far for me to walk back home at night, after grandma got the message that summer, saying I had to start visiting again on Saturdays!

It hadn't taken long for my mother's few pieces of furniture to be moved from one house to the other. I don't think she expected anything else to be put in bedrooms, apart from beds. She never had a dressing table, just a stand chair, to hold cigarettes, matches, and a candle. Her new home consisted of the front room that wasn't used at all until my dad came out of the army. A cold room, with a small tiled fireplace, where a fire was never lit. A brown three piece suite, a sideboard, a small table under the window, looked like most front rooms in Lancashire.

The back room, come living room, kitchen, bathroom and laundry, was furnished with a table, two stand chairs, a green kitchenette, and an armchair by the black iron fireplace. A gas oven stood by the back door, leading into the yard where the toilet was. These items, together with a clothes boiler, lit by the gas jet beneath it, made up the living room. It was not cosy or comfortable. Perhaps my mother thought it was, and at least she was under her own roof. Probably, through lack of space, chairs were very few in those small homes. Children stood at the table for their meals. Parents sat down.

My mother would not have coal kept in the backyard. She complained to the coalman, that it got so wet, she couldn't light the fire with it.

The coalman carried the sacks of coal through into the house, and throwing them over his shoulder, emptied them one by one, in the living room, under the stairs. There was coal dust everywhere! When he'd gone, an old brown velvet curtain, that had once been a table cloth, was pulled across, on a wire to hide it all.

'It's easy to get at, and nobody can pinch it there,' said my mother.

I started to go down early on Saturday mornings. It had become my job to order the potato pies and gravy from Jenning's Pie Shop, on the range. Orders for dinnertime, that meant twelve noon, had to be in before ten – o- clock in the morning. If you got there after ten, a notice would be in the shop window – 'No more orders for pies today!' The order for pies had to be written on a piece of paper with your name on. I always wrote, *'I want 3 potato pies, and gravy, please. A pie each for me and my mother, and half a pie for my two little sisters. Joyce.'* I never forgot the 'please'.

When I collected them at dinnertime, I stood in the long queue, with a dish I'd taken for the pies, and a jug for the gravy. Mr. Jennings came from the kitchen at the back of the shop – shouting 'Three Potato Pies with gravy for Joyce!' He put the pies in my dish, and filled the jug with gravy. The smell was delicious! The pies were golden brown, with jelly that hadn't quite set. The gravy, rich, thick and hot! Out of my mother's money, I sneaked tuppence out of the change, and bought myself a cream bun to eat on the way back to her house.

The rest of the morning, I'd spend going to Mr. Jones's 'selling out' shop. I cannot remember my mother shopping, but I became an expert at it!

Poor Mr. Jones never did get used to reading my mother's shopping lists. It took him ages to decipher what she wanted. I never took any money. It was always the same message I gave him – 'My mother says will you book it?'

'I suppose so, little un.' He'd say.

Even though I took the items home that she'd written on the list, it was never right. Packets were either too big or too small. She complained about 'Plum' jam, when she'd written 'Plum' jam. Biscuits were always 'Nice', because she always wrote – 'Some nice biscuits,' expecting Mr. Jones to think to himself – now what kind of biscuits would Annie like this week? But he didn't – and just sent a packet of 'Nice' biscuits. She would pick up the biscuits, looking at me, and say, 'He's sent these bloody biscuits again! He always sends the same ones! Why don't you tell him?'

My mother shopped 'in bits'. She bought food daily, but as people did not have fridges then; perhaps she had a point.

Sometimes my dad came home for a night. He was based at Preston, a few miles from Blackburn. He stole an army lorry to come home in, and hid it in the back, behind the houses. He told us to keep it a secret! Nobody had to know it was there! If dad came at weekend, I ordered five Potato Pies.

I hated the time when it was time for him to go back. I didn't like 'Goodbyes.' I hadn't experienced many, as people had been wrenched out of my life, so abruptly, I'd hardly felt the hurt. But I had seen so many 'Goodbyes' on the cinema screen, that I almost thought I had to cry if someone left me. So when it was time for my dad to go back, I felt so sad, I left the house, and walked down the range, until I thought he had gone. Sometimes I saw his army lorry drive away; then I would go back.

'You have missed your dad. He's gone!' was all my mother said.

Not only had I to visit my mother on Saturdays, I now had to visit her family as well. After we'd eaten our pies, my mother got my two younger sisters ready, and we set off to begin the walk from Freme Street to Riley Street. They had moved from Florence Street some time ago. We took the route along the 'bottom,' that was by the river, up Brookhouse Lane, a very steep hill, and across Whalley New Road, where the trams passed us, going to Blackburn Market. Up Birley Street, that seemed endless for my small legs, and tiring, because I had to help to push the pram with my sisters in, onto Eanam; then up to Audley – and to my other grandma's.

On our way, we passed houses, garages, corner shops, pubs, warehouses, foundrys and mills. Men in cloth caps, old ladies wrapped in black shawls, whatever the weather, sat on chairs outside of their houses, smoking pipes, or knitting. Some of the old ladies smoking pipes as well as the men.

A colourful and interesting display of life in a Lancashire town, that I would, one day, look back on with affection.

Riley Street was a writer and artist's dream! All Catherine Cookson's novels could have been rolled into one there. Lowry could have sat and drawn characters from life, to his heart's content.

As for me- I was introduced to a world quite apart from my grandma's, or the houses I'd seen on the silver screen.

Overcrowding must have been the worst bugbear for those families who lived as many as ten to a four roomed house. Mainly Catholic, they did what the Good Lord, or the local Irish Priest expected of them, and produced child upon child, until the wives either refused to sleep with their husbands, or tried all kinds of ways of using contraception, such as putting a cork from a bottle inside of themselves, or a lump of cotton wool soaked in Dettol, before letting their husbands come near them. The conversations between women chatting together on their front doorsteps, were often about what and what not to do, in order not to conceive. Names of back street abortionists were available, if trying to 'get rid of it' hadn't succeeded. Husbands were known to have raped their wives! To some women war came as a relief – from the pregnancies and miscarriages that brought them down in health, if it didn't kill them.

All this, I would learn later, but for now, going to 'my other grandma,' was just something I had to do. The house was really crowded when we got there. No sooner had we walked in, that we were out in the street again – me looking after my two sisters.

My mother's mother always sat at the table in the back room. She would be peeling huge amounts of potatoes, or darning a pile of socks. A comfortable plump woman, with jet black hair pulled back into a bun. She never said much to me, except for the one thing she would say every time I went there – Looking up from whatever she was doing, she would look at me and say, 'You're going to be a lady when you grow up, aren't you?' Although the other members of the family who happened to be there, laughed, I didn't appreciate the sarcasm in those early years, and answered, very seriously, 'Yes,' to which they would all laugh even more. Perhaps it was because I spoke better than a lot of children. I spoke Lancashire, but I didn't drop my aitches, and I used the words please and thank you a lot.

Little by little I learned the names of my aunts and Uncles who were new to me. Uncle Jim, married to Aunt Violet, was in the navy. A jolly fellow, who became Chief Supervisor at a mental institution after the war. Uncle Herbert, a cheerful bachelor. Uncle Milton, in his teens, good looking with slightly ginger hair, and a cheeky smile, who sadly, years later, would go to Ireland as a young soldier, and be blown to pieces by the I.R.A.

Aunt Dorothy, the eldest of the three sisters, who married her sweetheart, Charlie. I got on with them all quite well. Some, because they didn't speak much, or, like my Uncle John, kept out of the way. My mother's dad kept out of the way. He was either in the pub or in bed! Bernard, the youngest of the family, and a few years older than me, looked like my mother, with his dark curly hair and deep blue eyes. I only watched him from a distance, as I didn't like boys at the best of times!

My mother and her middle sister always seemed to have secrets to talk about. She was married, and had two small children, a boy and a girl, my new cousins. Their daddy too, was away at war.

Whoever my mother spoke to, with her family, her sister, or the neighbours in our street, it always seemed to be private and confidential when I was around.

Even on the coldest days, when visiting her family, they would start to talk; then glance at me. I got to know the cue!

My mother would say, 'Big Ears! Outside!'

I then went and sat on the front door step, until it was time to go to the chip shop for a massive amount of chips for the family tea. We children ate them standing at the table, deciding who would have a fork, and who would eat them with their fingers.

Sitting outside on the doorstep, I didn't mind, as I usually had my 'Sunny Stories' book, or 'Chick's Own' comic with me. What I did mind were the dead cockroaches on the vestibule floor! I would take a flying leap over them when I went back into the house.

If Uncle Jim was on leave, he would ask me to sing. I sang ' Bluebirds Over The White Cliffs of Dover,' for him and Violet. When I finished, they all clapped.

We stayed until most of mother's family got ready to go wherever they were going on Saturday night. Our grandma put on her best white blouse, and her navy blue coat. We walked with her to the pub on the corner. Here she joined her friends for her only bit of freedom of the week. There we left them, to walk back home to Freme Street. My mother must have felt a bit out of things. She was only twenty six years of age, and had her wings clipped early.

Saturday was a long day, and I was always pleased to be back at home with my grandma at 235!

## CHAPTER TEN

'You are changing schools,' said my grandma. 'We have got a letter from the school doctor. You're going to Blackamoor Open Air School after the summer holidays!'

Out came all the protestations I could think of. 'I can't! I don't know anybody! I don't know where it is! I won't like it!' Even though I didn't like Whalley Range School, or any school for that matter, I didn't think changing it would make my life any better. 'Why have I got to?' I moaned. 'The doctor says so. It's because you keep turning yellow,' grandma explained. Even though I said I wouldn't do it again, I was leaving my present school, and going to another in a few weeks time.

'You'll love it. It's out in the country, and you will get big and strong there,' I was told.

Children weren't taken along and introduced to the teacher in those days. If your name was down – you went!

I drifted along through the summer, getting more and more useful to my mother, and going to see her, if it could be called that, more and more often.

That summer I met Letty!

She was to play a big part in my life during the next few years. Small, but taller than me, with an elfin look, and short thick black hair, her sharp brown eyes took everything in. She was just as street wise as I would learn to be. A year older, and a bit more knowing, she would teach me a lot.

She was an only child, living with her parents at the top of

Freme Street, about ten doors away from us. They were not very well off, but had a nice home, and Letty had a lovely bedroom all to herself. Her dad, a quiet type wasn't in the army because he had a bad leg. Her mother, a bright little thing, always cheery, was welcoming to me when Letty took me in.

We stood together on the warm evenings, listening to the chit chat of the women of the street, standing at their doors. Letty knew all the scandal! She told me the woman who lived next door to them, had a baby while her husband was in the navy. He was wounded, and was sent home. When he found out about the baby, he went mad! He told his wife, 'Right! If that's what you want – you can have it!' and he made her do 'Thingy' every night!

Whatever 'Thingy' was that he made her do, Letty didn't say, and I didn't ask, but it sounded very serious!

My new friend was a bit of a Tomboy, and mixed in better than I did with the crowd of children who congregated at the bottom of the street, mainly because she could play cricket as good as any boy, climb a wall quicker, and always hit the ball when we played 'Rounders' in the street. She could stand on her hands by the wall, and would not mind showing her knickers. She could juggle three balls, while I struggled with two. She could run fast, ride a bike, and would accept any dare from the boys to go across the river Blakewater, that ran along the bottom of the street, and to climb through the broken windows of the dark derelict mill on the other side. Although the river was only a few feet wide at that point, sometimes it was quite rapid, and only a few times did I take up the dare to follow her. I was glad when the American soldiers were based in the mill, and it became strictly out of bounds.

We collected and swapped pictures of film stars. She gave

me a proper photo of Tyrone Power, that I kept, showing it to everyone, telling them it was my dad! Lettie's mother bought the magazine called 'Picturegoer', so it was easy for Letty to collect photos of film stars. Sometimes we went to the local cinemas to ask if we could have the old posters that hung in the foyer, advertising the films. Only if they were torn or stained did they give them to us. 'The are kept for the archives,' we were told.

We swapped problems as little girls do. Letty told me some things she made me promise never to tell anyone, so I never did! I told her I didn't know where I was going to live. I told her I didn't like going to Mr. Jones's shop. I didn't like school. I didn't like going visiting up Riley Street on Saturdays.

'If you have to come back and live with your mother, you will have me!' she said.


Three double decker buses waited on Blackburn Boulevard every weekday morning at 8.30, to take the weaker and more delicate children of the town, the fifteen minute journey in to the country to Blackamoor Open Air School. Some asthmatic, some convalescing from childhood ailments, or operations, or more serious illnesses, such as rheumatic fever or diphtheria. Some just suffering from plain neglect and malnutrition, and one – who kept turning yellow!

With a box hanging on a cord round my neck, containing my gas mask, my name and address, and 2/1d for my dinner money, my grandad left me in the bus queue on September morning, along with the other children.


A wonderful school! In its own grounds, separate classrooms, composed of mainly large glass windows, looked out on beautifully tended gardens. It was the best of schools, with special and the kindest of teachers.

Health wise, we were given milk in the morning and afternoon, or for a treat, hot chocolate or Ovaltine. Malt was given out by the monitor of the week, who came round the class with a huge white enamel jug, brimming with thick bubbly malt. The monitor would dip a clean teaspoon into the malt, bring it out, and wrap the delicious stuff round and round the spoon; then hand it to you. If the monitor was a friend of yours, you would get an extra large spoonful. If that week you happened to be the monitor, and we all got a turn, then you got to scrape out the jug, and guzzle yourself, before taking it back to the kitchen.

Iron tonic was given out to us by Nurse Kelly. As we left the dining room after lunch, she handed each of us a small green egg cup, containing the tonic. It was brown and tasted a little bit bitter. We had to drink it; then hand her back the egg cup, saying, 'Thank you, Nurse Kelly.'

After lunch we made our way outside into the playgrounds. Large open fronted sheds were placed at one side, where we slept or rested on small folding beds, wrapped in our thick grey individual blankets, that we kept in our individual lockers. My locker was number 112. Most of the children slept for an hour, but if not, we had to lay quietly. On no account were we allowed to speak. The teacher on 'rest duty' sat watching over us. She sat in a deck chair, herself wrapped in blankets, especially on a cold wintry day.

If children arrived at school feeling poorly, they reported to Nurse Kelly, who placed a folding bed in the main corridor, across from the dining room. Next to the radiators, it was warm and cosy. I was placed in a bed for the day now and then. It was usually on Fridays when the cook was making cheese pie in the kitchen, and the smell, that I could not stand, wafted through the school, making me feel sick. I detested school lunches. Tastes that were new to me, like beetroot and spinach, repulsed me, and cheese pie with onions, I could not face at all. I put it in my pockets, in my shoes, anywhere to get rid of it when Nurse Kelly wasn't looking. I was quite in awe of her during my first year at the school. She was small and chubby. Her dark hair pulled back under her flowing white nurses cap, she reminded me, in looks, like my mother's mother. She spoke with a slight Irish accent, and I couldn't always understand what she said. She called me 'Paleface,' which I suppose was a term of affection, but when I told my mother this, she said, 'Tell her you're not a bloody red Indian!' which didn't help. Many months on, I was to become one of Nurse Kelly's girls! Meaning, helping in the surgery every morning, and being given treats, like going for tea at her house in Dukes Brow at Christmas time.

At Blackamoor Open Air School I shone! I could read so well, I helped the non readers when we sat in groups for reading practice. I was good at drama and verse speaking. I was soon given a place in the school choir. I was to sing in the town's music festival in the springtime, and chosen to play the part of the Virgin Mary in the nativity play in December. For months we rehearsed this, and I loved the afternoons I was called out of class to try on my lovely blue and white voile dress and headgear, and to sing to 'baby Jesus,' the carol, ' Hush My Dear, Lie Still and Slumber,' even if I didn't believe in him!

I was not so fond of P.E, that we seemed to have a lot of, outside in the fresh air, but I enjoyed the nature walks we took in the countryside. The showers we took on Thursdays were great fun, when Nurse Kelly looked at our skin and in our hair. Of course, I hadn't got nits – not with my grandma around!

Part of the extensive grounds were divided into small plots, each child having their own piece of land to plant vegetables and flowers. All the vegetables I hated eating, I loved growing, and the flowers that bloomed could be taken home, or used to decorate the school if something special was happening.

The only thing none of us children liked, was when the caravan came! Twice a year a great white caravan parked between the classrooms. In it – was Nurse Totty from the clinic in the town – and with her – The Dentist! Dental treatment was carried out in the caravan to prevent the trauma of having to attend the 'school clinic.' We were lovingly treated, given warm milk, and allowed to lie in our little beds in the warm corridors after, we all still hated the sight of that caravan!

The war was seldom mentioned to us at school. We had 'gas mask' and 'air raid' drill, where we all put on our gas masks, and walked in single file to the underground air raid shelter. We went down the steps into the darkness of the dug out mound, that contained forms for us to sit on. It was lit inside with tiny lamps. Mr. Heaps, our school caretaker had made cupboards, to hold books, drinks, blankets, and things that Nurse Kelly might need for the children who felt ill. We never stayed in there very long, and sang songs to while away the time, and keep us from being afraid.

Miss Wilkinson, our headmistress, received food parcels from the American soldiers, to be distributed among the children. We stood in the hall, and went up to Miss Wilkinson one by one, when she handed us something nice out of the parcels. Sometimes I would get a tin of drinking chocolate, or a tin of corned beef, or spam to take to my mother. If we were given cookies, or sweets, we ate them on our way home!

Each morning grandad took me down to the boulevard on the tramcar, to get my bus. Before the tram stopped at the terminus, just outside of Woolworth's, he would scoop me up in his arms, and jump off the tram as it was still moving. I suppose it was a dangerous thing to do, and he got a few dirty looks from the other passengers. Neither of us ever mentioned it to grandma - but I loved it!

Grandma not only visited Blackburn market on Saturdays, she also went there on Wednesdays, coming home with all sorts of goodies she knew we enjoyed. Creamy oat cakes we spread thinly with our butter ration. A bag of broken biscuits, from the boy with ginger hair who worked on the biscuit stall in the market house. All colours of knitting wools, and remnants of materials, that she would make up into a simple dress for me, or a new coat and bonnet for 'Rosebud'. On Wednesday afternoons she met me off the bus that brought me from school, and as a treat we would go to the 'Hake Boat' – a super little café, near to the boulevard. Pictures of a wavy blue sea, with fish and boats decorated the window, while inside they served the best fish and chips in Lancashire. We sat at a table for two, with a red check tablecloth on it, a huge salt cellar, next to a bottle of vinegar.

Grandma wore her little black astrakhan hat and her mother of pearl earrings in the shape of two tiny love birds. We enjoyed our tea together, before we got the tramcar to go back home. Wednesdays became special.

During the transfer to my new school, my mother had been away for a few weeks, and I was spared the visits and the trauma of walking back home in the dark. I'd picked up in overheard conversations that she had taken my two young sisters somewhere 'down south'. She had been to Haywards Heath to see my dad, who was stationed there. It meant little to me when I heard that he had got engaged to a girl called Betty, and my mother had gone to tell her he was married with three children!

Whatever he'd done at the time, had given me a break – but now she was back home, and my Saturday routine had started again, as well as having to go to her house to 'run errands' two nights a week, after school.

I told Letty what my dad had done, and she crossed her heart and promised not to tell anyone.

By now my dad was posted back up to Preston, and came home on leave more often in his stolen truck.

Sometimes I stayed all night at my mother's. On these nights, when he was home, they went out to the pub.

I was to learn that my dad was a 'Billy Liar', though then I did not know the meaning of the word. I also didn't know that men could sew – but my dad could! Before he went out with my mother to the local pub, he took a long time to get ready – not only did he polish his army boots till they shone, and his buttons. Pressed his trousers with a hot iron and a wet cloth, put Brylcream on his hair, and touched up his moustache with a little bit of soot from the chimney breast, but sewed, very meticulously, three stripes onto the arm of the sleeve of his army uniform! Next morning he would cut them off carefully. They were put in a small cardboard box in the top drawer of the sideboard, in the front room, until he came home, and went to the pub next time.

A bomb had dropped on Blackburn!

It was the first and last bomb to be dropped on our

smokey little town, that the Germans had drawn out on their maps as a lake. It wasn't during an air raid, when families were sitting under their stairs in candlelight, or in their cold, grey corrugated roofed Anderson shelters. It was, my grandma said, 'a sneaky little bomb.'

The Blackburn Telegraph newspaper reported it. Preston docks had been bombed that evening, and the German pilot, on his way home, flew his plane over Blackburn. He spotted a solitary light, flickering on and off, and travelling in one direction. He followed the flickering light. When it stopped, he dropped a bomb, not even knowing what the light was.

All the good people of Blackburn could have told him what it was – It was the last tramcar, usually the ten o clock, making its way from Wilpshire to the centre of Blackburn. No one but the driver and the conductor were aboard, as it made its way past my grandma's house at 235. The over head electric trolley cable flickered in the darkness of the night sky. It was when the driver turned the familiar corner by the river Blakewater, and stopped the tram, the light flickered for the last time. The bomb killed them both!

Windows were blown out of surrounding pubs and shops. The huge plate glass ones of Woolworths, helped to litter the road around the great black hole and the carnage the bomb had produced.

In the cold light of morning the roads were cordoned off, as people gathered to view the scene, as people will.

I passed this unfamiliar sight a couple of days later, on one of the mornings I walked to the boulevard to get my bus to school, after staying at my mother's house overnight. The scene was like it was on the films – buildings with no windows, wood, glass and stones littering the pavements. Shrapnel had made small dents in the walls, just like someone had thrown heavy stones, and scarred badly, the lovely pale marble walls of the Royal Cinema near by. The picture frames that had held posters and photos of the film stars advertising the current films showing that week, were cracked and broken.

The tram terminus was moved for a while – and never again would my grandad jump off the tram with me under his arm.

# CHAPTER ELEVEN

The boys congregated at the corner of Freme Street, showing off, telling jokes, playing cricket, and all the things mentionable and not, that boys congregating on corners do.

'Do you got to Penks or do you go to Charnleys?' they asked Letty and me. Not knowing what they were talking about, I said nothing. Letty answered them – 'We go to Penks. Charnleys is a flea pit!'

Like so many things, Letty then explained to me – Penks and Charnleys were two cinemas, each on a corner very near to Riley Street where I trailed to see my mother's family every Saturday afternoon. Charnleys was a smaller building than Penks, painted on the outside in a deep pea green colour. Penks looked more like a proper cinema from the outside, painted in brown and cream. 'They have to be painted in those colours,' Letty told the boys on the corner, 'It's camouflage!' She often came out with big words I didn't know, and didn't ask about, but I knew the boys thought she was clever.

I hadn't visited Penks or Charnleys. It was Letty's bright idea that if I went with her on Saturday afternoons, I could still visit the family in Riley Street, that was only round the corner, but not have to stay there so long, as being at the pictures would take up most of the time.

So from then on, my visits to my mother's family were cut short. They were probably glad to get rid of 'big ears' listening in to their conversations, and as I had to take my younger sister to Penks with me, that was another body less in their overcrowded home. As long as I got back to the house in time to go to the chip shop for the massive order of chips for tea – everyone seemed happy.

When I'd been at home at my grandma's on Friday nights, she would give me the three pennies I needed to pay to get in the cinema, and a few sweets to take with me. If I stayed at my mother's on Friday night, that was becoming usual, rather than ask her for the money, I pinched a penny out of the change when I went for the pies and gravy. Letty gave me a penny, and the other penny I got by taking empty jam jars back to the local grocer, who gave me a halfpenny each for them.

If I could dodge out of the house for a while, avoiding my mother's orders to go on numerous errands, Saturday morning, with Letty, could be quite profitable. We would knock on the doors of the neighbours, and ask them if they had any empty jam jars or bottles. Sometimes they saved them for us.

We stood in the noisy queue of children outside of the cinema doors, sometimes in the poring rain. Children dropped into the habit of queuing very quickly, when it became a ministerial order in the year of 1942 – when people should form orderly queues when shopping for food, so all could get their fair share of rations. They queued to get into the air raid shelters when the siren sounded, to get on the trams, or to be seen by the doctor. 'It made good sense,' said my grandad. 'It's only good manners,' said my grandma.

Eventually the cinema doors opened, and we filed in, handing our three pennies to the lady locked in her little kiosk, who gave each one of us a small pink ticket, that we immediately dropped onto the floor. Once inside the dimness and warmth, we surged to where we all thought the best seats were. The man in charge, dressed in his tatty uniform, with a piece of gold braid on his shoulder and round his flat hat, banged the big cane he carried, against the back of the seats. It sounded with a piercing crack, as he ordered us to 'sit down', in his loud booming voice.

The Pictorial Newsreel wasn't shown on Saturday afternoon, and we settled down to watch Donald Duck or Mickey Mouse, in colour. Then the serial – 'Queen of the Jungle.' The lady actress in this was lovely. Although the film was in black and white, she had black shiny marcel waved hair, and large eyes. She wore a white safari suite, as she ran away from crocodiles and snakes, waded through polluted waters, and spoke softly to baby monkeys. Just as she was getting into deathly danger, the film came to a close, and the words - MORE NEXT WEEK AT THIS CINEMA......flashed onto the screen. We all said 'OH!' in unison.

After the few minutes interval, when the boys made as much noise as possible, and threw apple stumps and various things over our heads – the big film came on. Bob Hope in 'Road to Morocco', Bing Crosby in 'Going My Way.' Laurel and Hardy, or 'Lasssie.' We didn't care what film it was. Letty and me closed our eyes when the credits came on. She peeped through her fingers. 'When it says 'directed by' she told us, 'then the film starts.' – and it always did!

In the boring bits of the film, when men were talking together, and we couldn't understand what they were talking about, we went to the toilet.

When the film broke and we were plunged into darkness, that happened nearly every week, we all stamped our feet, and shouted – 'Put a penny in' gas!' – that made the man in charge come down the aisles waving his stick to shut us up.

If an actor with a German accent came into the film, we would all shout 'Boo!' If the King and Queen came on, or the princesses, we all cheered. At the end of the performance, the National Anthem was played, and the wide doors of the cinema opened, letting in the bright day light. Before the Anthem had finished, we were all out of the cinema, and the doors shut behind us.

Letty went home. I went to get the chips for tea.

Things were changing at Riley Street. My mother's mother had become very ill. She lay in a single bed that had been brought down from upstairs, and put in the corner of the living room, next to the fireplace. The bed took up most of the room, and the house was even more crammed. My mother's elder sister did her best to manage the large family, do the cooking, washing, and caring of their mother day and night. Well meaning neighbours walked in and out, whispering in loud voices. I listened to what they said – 'She has dropsy. She has a tired heart. She looked bad, worse than last week! She hadn't long. Poor Mary! She's had a rotten life. She's only 53!'

They were right! Very soon after, she died.

It was a strange feeling, going into the house again, and seeing her in her coffin in the front room. The curtains were drawn together over the window, and there was a gentle hush in the house, so different from the usual bustle and chatter. My mother's elder sister stood by the coffin as people walked in and out quietly to take a last look at Mary and pay their respects. Her pale face and jet black hair, neatly brushed to the back of her head, was covered with a square of soft white muslin, that our Auntie removed and replaced gently, while people came and went. This grandmother, who I never regarded as my grandmother, was the first dead person I had seen. I sensed the sorrow of the family who loved her, as I stood on the outside feeling little emotion – but did think she was quite old at 53!

I related the story of it all, bit by bit, to my grandma, when I got home. She didn't comment at any time. Whatever I told her about the family on 'the other side' of town, she would just nod – saying nothing.

I didn't hear anything about the funeral. My mother didn't speak to me about it, and I didn't ask. I asked my mother very little about anything.  We abruptly stopped going to Riley Street on Saturdays. So I abruptly stopped going to Penks as well. Letty said, 'not to worry, we could start going to the Rialto Cinema instead. They gave you free sweets and a drink of pop at Christmas.' Occasionally, my mother took us to see one of her other sisters. I tried when I could, to get out of going. When I was made to go, it meant looking after my sisters, pushing the youngest one up and down the streets in her pram. I was always told to go outside – as though I was interested in their stupid secrets!

My mother's dad was never popular with his children. He hadn't been a good husband. He got married again some time later – to a woman who lived further up Riley Street. His family were bemused, and didn't bother with him. He'd never done a stroke of housework in his life – but was seen scrubbing the front doorstep of the home of his second wife – much to their satisfaction!

Among grandma's many sayings, such as, 'People die in bed.' 'It will either rain or go dark before morning.' 'Since

Adam was a lad' or, if she didn't feel well – 'A good run round the block might make me better!' One of her regular sayings to me, on Sunday, was – 'If you are good, you can dirty your dress out tomorrow.' That meant – on Monday I could wear my Sunday dress for school, if I had kept it clean enough. We had weekday clothes and clothes we kept for 'best' to wear on Sundays or on special occasions.

Not having to wear a school uniform until we got to secondary school, gave the girls a chance to show off their Sunday dresses on Monday, that's if they had one! Mine was usually homemade. Miss Muffet Print material, worn with a darker coloured knitted cardigan that didn't show the dirt. Some girls came to school wearing fancy dresses with frills and puffed sleeves. I wasn't a flouncy and frilly person – but I think I would have liked to have been.

Grandad had stopped firewatching at the abattoirs for some reason, and with the coming of the long winter evenings, plied me with encyclopaedias to read, and played knowledgeable games with me and grandma. 'Bird, Fish, Flower, Fruit, Vegetable, Animal, Town and River' was a favourite. We all found the name of each one beginning with the letter'A'; then worked our way through the alphabet. Of course grandad always won!

We listened to the Strauss waltzes and songs sung by Richard Tauber. 'You are My Heart's Delight' and 'One Alone' came through the speaker of the old gramophone grandad had to keep winding up, as the music and songs slowed down, making funny sounds. Grandma would let them run down just to have a laugh. We played 'Poor Old Rover' on a worn and well loved record, when we sat silently to hear the recorded story about the dog who lost his master, and went to sit on his grave, until he too died. Grandma always had tears in her sad brown eyes at the end, so I did as well.

These evenings were precious – but not to last.

My mother had gone back to work in the mill, and I was needed more and more after school, to light the fire before she got home at 5.30 in the evening, collect my young sisters from the neighbour next door but one; then to do the errands.


It was time to put on the nativity play at school.

The main hall was packed with pupils and staff, as well as parents and important visitors from the Town Hall and the Education Offices. A man with a big camera on a tripod was there from the Blackburn Times newspaper – It was wonderful!

We all played our parts magnificently. The angel Gabriel, a girl called Pauline, stood behind me, dressed in white, holding a stick with a golden star stuck on it. The Kings and Shepherds came upon the stage and sat among the pot lambs, and the choir sang in the background. Then when all went quite – a ray of light shone onto me, in my soft blue and white gown, while I sang 'Hush my Dear, Lie still and Slumber' – in my best voice. I gently rocked the cradle, although this was rather difficult to do, as the boy playing Jesus was little and fat, and I had to be careful not to tip him over. He sat in the cradle for a long time, and his nose was running. Miss Wilkinson said, 'Never mind! We were all wonderful, and a credit to the school.' The audience clapped and clapped, and a man from the Town Hall gave a speech, but none of us remembered what he said.

Nobody I knew came to see the play. Grandma's legs were bad, and the journey to the school in the cold weather would have been too much for her. I didn't tell my mother about the play. She saw the photo in the newspaper the following week – with little comment. But Nurse Kelly said – 'Well done, Little Paleface!' – and that meant a lot.

Grandma bustled her way through the month of December, icing her Christmas cakes, finishing them off by placing a tiny robin or artificial snowman on top. She placed them along the top of the sideboard, to be covered with a white table cloth. A week later they were distributed to certain members of her family, her sisters and Henry her brother, who'd parted from his wife. She made a small one for Miss Warburton, next door, one for Polly and Maggie, her friends, and of course, one for us.

She'd knitted and sewn garments throughout the autumn, to give as presents, and wrapped them in festive wrapping paper she had saved from the year before. The chicken was on order from the Co-op shop, to be cooked on Christmas morning. Her mince pies were ready in a tin, waiting to be sprinkled with icing sugar, and the milkman who came round with his horse and cart, had promised her a drop of real cream for the trifle we would have for tea. Grandad had got his usual round box full of chocolate liquors, wrapped in all colours of shiny paper. Every year, he teased grandma, saying he hadn't been able to get them, then on Christmas Eve he brought them out. She always pretended to be surprised – but I think she knew!

Even though my grandparents did not see my sisters, grandma always made sure a small gift was sent for them, that I would take.

It was to be a special Christmas that year, as Auntie Rene had bought four tickets for the pantomime at the Grand

Theatre on Christmas Eve. It was a small, but cosy and
friendly theatre, with red plush seats. The stage was adorned
with thick velvet curtains, maroon, with gold fringing. I had
only been inside once before, but imagined myself, one day,
singing on the stage. That night I was going to see 'Cinderella',
and there was to be a real coach to take her to the ball. I was
going to sit in the balcony with my aunts, Rene, Eva, and my
cousin Averil

I'd spent the day going errands for my mother and Alice.
I'd played with my sisters, keeping them from under my
mother's feet. At four in the afternoon, I asked if I could go.
'Not yet!' my mother said. Grandma had told me to go home
early. She knew I didn't like the darkness and the loneliness of
the streets when the shops had closed, and that night was
special, as we had to get a tramcar early, to take us into town,
so as not to be late for the theatre.

I watched the clock move on, and asked again. 'Can I go
now?' My mother said, each time I asked, 'Not yet!' I was
getting anxious, and although I did not protest about things
with my mother, I told her, what she already knew – 'We are
going to the pantomime tonight.'

'Are you now?' she replied. Alice listened in.

'I'm going to be very late. Grandma said I should be back
home early,' I said as politely as I could.

'Really!' was all she said.

By now I was feeling distraught. I suppose I should have
burst into tears. I didn't. I waited, knowing my grandma
would be standing at her front door, watching out for me. In
the meantime I was watching my mother and Alice, and they
were watching me. No way would I cry in front of those two!

It was about six thirty when the knock came on the front

door. Alice and my mother exchanged glances, before my mother went to open the door. I knew it would be my Auntie Rene. I would be able to go now. I heard her say, 'I've come for 'our Pip' – that was her pet name for me.

My best green coat hung on a peg behind the back door. I got it down and put it on. I was ready!

'Have you now?' I heard my mother say. The conversation became muffled as Alice went to the front door to join my mother, closing the middle door behind her. Voices were being raised. I opened the middle door and walked towards them. My Auntie Rene held out her hand, saying, 'Come on Pip love. We are late already.' My mother turned to me and pointed her finger at me. 'You! In! Now!' she ordered. Turning her back to me, she shouted to my aunt, 'Your Pip, as you call her, is going nowhere!' As I went back into the kitchen, I heard Alice having her say – 'She's staying where she belongs,' she was shouting. It seemed to go quiet for a few moments, before I heard the slapping and screaming and swearing. They were fighting! All at once my Auntie shouted, 'It will all be alright Pip love! Don't worry!' Suddenly the front door shut with a bang. My mother and Alice came back in to the house looking dishevelled. Swearing, and saying they would 'take the whole bloody lot of them to court.'

My mother looked at me. I'd taken off my green coat and hung it up again behind the back door. Her words were few. She jerked her thumb. 'You! Upstairs!' It was too early to go to bed, even on Christmas Eve. I knew I was going nowhere that night. I meekly went upstairs, and sat on the edge of the single bed I would be sharing with my younger sister. I listened to as much conversation going on downstairs between them as I could stand, then covered my ears with my hands and fell asleep. I knew Father Christmas wouldn't be coming to me, because Alice had told me he didn't exist, the year before.

During the morning of that Christmas day that would alter the course of my life, a neighbour called. 'There's a parcel on your doorstep,' she said. My mother brought it in. It was addressed to me. In it were clean clothes, a few Christmas presents, things I needed for school, a slice of homemade Christmas cake, and a letter from my grandma….

'It will all be sorted when your dad comes home; then you can go to a singing teacher and have your voice trained. Don't worry. Be a good girl….'

When the new school term started, I half knew my grandma would meet me off the school bus on Wednesday – and she did. We went into the Hake Boat café for tea, but we couldn't eat. We looked at each other and broke down into tears. When she left she hugged me, and gave me the brown paper carrier bag she'd brought. 'They're are the rest of your things,' she said. Neither of us said 'Goodbye' as we swallowed the lump in our throats. My grandma got on the tramcar. I watched it wind its way into Penny Street, and out of sight.

I ran all the way back to my mother's house. I was late! The fire needed to be lit before she got home from the mill.

Grandma must have been sent a message from my mother. Although I waited outside of the Hake Boat on Wednesdays, she did not come to meet me anymore.

I didn't see her again for two years.

## CHAPTER TWELVE

To question the right, as a child, to be given a roof over your head by your parents, to be given food and clothing, shouldn't occur. It didn't occur to me that I should 'work' for a living. Perhaps my grandma had 'spoiled' me, as the saying goes. I'd helped in the house, by dusting the piano legs, and places that my grandma couldn't get down to, ironed the hankies, shelled the peas, and gone to the Co-op shop for the odd item, but never had I cleaned the toilet, emptied the jerries, lit fires, or stoned steps.

School became a release from my sadness –

It was warm at school, and apart from the school dinners, I enjoyed my days. If I didn't feel well, or Nurse Kelly noticed the dark rings under my eyes, I was put to bed on the corridor for the day. Teachers and pupils smiled at me as they passed. I was given hot milky drinks by the dinner ladies. It was the only place where I was shown any affection.

At least during that winter I had plenty of warm clothes. My grandma sent parcels to me containing vests, wool socks, cardigans, pixie bonnets, gloves, and a winter coat, as well as my crayons, paints, and books. I still had my pink fluffy dressing gown, that now, I wore in bed, in the cold unheated bedroom. I shared a single bed with my sister. When she wet the bed, she wet me as well.

I'd been able to wash and care for myself from the age of two, although my grandma had always washed my hair in Derbac soap. Now I washed my own hair with any kind of soap. I kept myself as clean as I could with the help of the shower we had at school on Thursday, and the visit to the public slipper baths in Belper Street, where I went with my sister, on Saturday afternoons. This ruled out my afternoon at the cinema with Letty.

On bad winter days, I hated the wind, sleet, and snow. I hated being cold, and promised myself that when I grew up, I would always be warm. I hated the long walk against the elements from Freme Street to the Boulevard, to meet the school bus each morning. Sometimes I met Miss Caine, a teacher at the school. She lived on Whalley Range, in one of the posher houses, with large bay windows, and steps leading up to the front door, through the garden. Small, lean and sensibly dressed in blouses with neat collars, hand knitted cardigans, and a no nonsense tweed winter coat, that matched her no nonsense tweed winter hat, that covered her short dark curly hair. She would meet me at the top of Freme Street, and we would walk together briskly to the boulevard, talking about sensible things. If I wanted to dawdle, or stop to look at the pictures of film stars behind the glass casements on the wall of the Royal Cinema, or if I wanted to call in to Mrs. Ward's toffee shop at the top of Ice Street, for a penny sherbet, or a penny bag of parched peas, I'd have to set off a few minutes earlier to avoid Miss Caine. That's if I could get my sisters ready in good time, and park them with the neighbour, who took them to their nursery school.

Letty became my confidante and adviser, telling me the things she would do if she were in my position. Her mother had felt sorry for me over Christmas, and had invited me for tea now and then, to stay round the fireside with them in the evenings. Sometimes my mother let me go, sometimes she didn't.

Letty said, 'If I was you, I would tell your mother and Alice to Bugger Off!' 'Would you really?' I asked her. I knew Letty was very brave.

'Yes I would! Next time they send you on all those errands – tell them!'

'Yes, I will!' I told her. But I didn't! When Letty asked if I had, I said, 'Well, I nearly did!'

The worst time of my day was the time between leaving school, and my mother coming home from the mill, just after five thirty. I could never get the fire to light. I did all the things I could think of to get it to go. I put the shovel up to it with a newspaper across, to create a draught underneath. I held the paper with my thumbs on each side, until it caught alight; then I had to push it into the firegrate, where it flew in flames up the chimney, but still the fire didn't light. My sisters were cold and hungry, and my mother cross and tired when she came in. Then it was time for me to go to the shops. We never seemed to have enough bread or milk. If I was sent to the chip shop, there would be a long queue. I was always in trouble when I got home, for taking such a long time.

If I had a halfpenny, I would ask the lady in the chip shop – 'Have you got a bag of bits please?' She would scrape all the bits of batter together that had dropped off the fish as they were cooking, and put them in a large white bag for me. I liberally sprinkled them with salt and vinegar, and ate them on my way home. Sometimes we had fried bread for tea, sometimes 'dippy egg' – a slice of bread, dipped in batter that had been made with dried egg powder and water. By seven o clock in the evening, the fire would just about be going. My sisters had to be washed in the sink, and put to bed. My days seemed long.

I didn't always go straight home after school. I took Letty's advice. Let them go their own bloody errands!

Just under Darwen Street Bridge, was a forge. A wonderful sight! As we passed it on the school bus, the children would get up from their seats, and surge to the windows on the left side to catch a glimpse of the man in his black leather apron, as he stood by the fire that roared and lit up the street. He struck and hammered the horse's shoes, sending sparks like small fireworks in all directions. Sometimes one of the great Shire horses, that pulled the carts containing the huge brown casks of beer from Thwaites Brewery, would be waiting to be shod. I loved that scene! So when I met a girl at school, called Jean, who lived very near to the forge, and who invited me round to her house for a jam butty, with all the other kids in her street, before her mother got home from work – I went! We stood at the entrance of the forge, watching in wonderment, while the heat penetrated through our small bones, making our faces glow. I was lucky then, to have gloves, but some of the children wore old socks on their hands.

Other times, I left the school bus, and walked across the busy roads of the boulevard, where buses and trams pulled in behind each other, to the man cooking baked potatoes in a big black cast iron oven. It was on wheels, and underneath, the man kept a small but fearsome fire burning, to keep the oven hot.

With fiddling my mother's change when doing the errands, and taking bottles and jam jars back to the shops, I usually had a copper or two in my pocket. I stood beside the hot oven, savoring the delicious smell of baking potatoes. When it was my turn, I said, 'Twopennyworth please.' The man put a few quartered potatoes in a white paper bag. 'Help yourself to salt, Love,' he said to every customer. I put my fingers into the big box of warm salt that balanced itself by the side of the oven, and sprinkled it on my potatoes. Eating them bit by bit, I walked slowly home.

I was always in trouble when I was late. 'Where do you think you've been? Why is the fire not lit? Why were these two young ones not collected? We need some milk. We need some bread.'

My excuses came easier and easier, - 'The bus broke down. A boy on the bus had a fit, and the teacher had to call an ambulance. I had to call at the school clinic on Victoria Street, and they made me wait.'

I was becoming as 'cute as a basket of Whelps,' said my mother.

I listened with Letty, to the boys standing at the corner of the street, where they gathered every night under the gas lamp in the winter months. They were bragging and boasting as usual. The new thing was how they could climb over the gate at the front of the Paper Mill, and get as far as the worksheds, where the heavy bales of paper were stored, without the night watchman seeing them. They always had some big scheme in mind, something illegal and dangerous – until they heard their mothers calling them in. Mothers shouted in the streets after their children when it was time for bed. 'Brian! Jimmy!' etc; would echo round the houses. The other children would also shout to the one whose name they could hear being called. 'You're wanted!' they would tell them. My mother would shout for me before my bedtime. She shouted for me to go home and put my sisters to bed. 'Don't answer,' said Letty. 'Don't go!'

Sometimes I didn't, and Letty and me ran off and hid, or walked along Whalley Range, arm in arm, looking in the shop windows.

It was on one of these evenings when Letty said to the boys on the corner – 'Who's going to see the Flasher on Sunday?' They all answered at once – 'I am!' She then turned to me, 'Are you coming to see the Flasher on Sunday?' 'What's a Flasher?' I asked. Well, the boys threw themselves about with laughter, slapping each other, putting their hands over their mouths, and rolling about on the floor, as boys do!

Letty whispered in my ear. I stood silent for a few moments, then asked her, 'What does he do that for? It's freezing cold!'

'Shut up!' said Letty. 'Are you coming or not?'

'Yes,' I said meekly.

After tea on Sunday, I managed to get out, after doing the washing up. I trailed with the rest of the gang through the backs behind William Herbert Street. Letty told me that only in streets like ours did Flashers 'hang out.' They didn't go in the posh areas.

After waiting a while – we saw him. He was tall and thin, wearing a long grey mac, with a flat cap on his head. Standing at a distance, well behind the others – I watched! The boys jeered, shouting insults, 'Does your mother only let you out on Sundays Dickie?' Letty shouted – 'Put it away! We've seen bigger Woodbines!' They all laughed, and I laughed, but what at, I don't know. I hadn't seen a thing! All of a sudden – he had gone.

I was going to sing in the Blackburn Music Festival. Mrs Williams, our music teacher, had chosen me, with two other girls, to represent our school. It was to be in April, in a large hall in Blakey Street, in the centre of town. The songs had been chosen. 'The Apple Elf' and 'The Windmill' were being rehearsed. I would rather have sung 'My Heart Awakes When April Sings' or 'Can't help Singing,' the songs Mrs Williams let me sing in front of the class after the singing lesson on Friday afternoons. I enjoyed being called out of the classroom during a lesson, to rehearse in the school dining room. Once, I went with the other girls to Mrs William's house in Buncer Lane, for extra rehearsals. She made tea and cake for us, served with those special little forks, the same as my grandma had. Everything was tidy in her beautiful home. She had lovely flowers in vases, and scented soap in her bathroom, where everything was pink. The towels were pink, and she even had a pink toilet roll. 'I am going to have a house like this when I grow up,' I told myself.

Miss Wilkinson, the headmistress, decided it would be nice if we three girls could sing in the festival, in dresses we had made ourselves, at school, of course. A soft sky blue cotton material was chosen. The teachers measured each of us, and cut out the pattern of the dresses, with a sweetheart neck, to be edged with white braid and small puffed sleeves. I don't remember making mine, or even touching it until it was almost ready to wear, when I was allowed to put a few stitches in the white braiding on the neckline. I think Mrs. Williams made my dress.

On the big day, we had to be at the hall at 2pm. There were twenty five girls singing in the class. We were not among the first to perform, but I was to be the first out of the three of us.

As a treat, we did not have to go into school that day. Miss Wilkinson said it would take us all morning to wash our hair, and make ourselves look pretty for the afternoon. She gave each of us a blue hair ribbon, and reminded us that we must have white ankle socks.

I hadn't got white ankle socks, but took my mother's word that I would have on the day.

During the morning, I washed my hair, and tied it back with my new blue ribbon. My mother was coming home from the mill at dinnertime, and we were going to go to Tunstall's Clothing Shop on Whalley Range, for my new white ankle socks. We could only buy from Tunstall's, or Haworth's in Montague Street, as they were the only shops that accepted clothing coupons, that my mother bought every week from a neighbour who ran a clothing club.

She was late coming home from the mill, and I was ready in my blue and white dress. I could not eat the potato pie she had brought for my dinner. I was too excited, and afraid that I might spill the gravy down me. I'd still got the black patent shoes that my mother had given to me some years ago. My sister wore them now, but I could just about get my feet into them, if I tried.

The clock ticked round. My mother had to be back at the mill by one-o-clock. We left home, and quickly walked up Freme Street and along the Range to Tunstalls. When we got to the shop door, the blind was down. A notice, stuck on the inside of the window stated 'Closed.' Most shopkeepers closed at dinnertime for an hour, this one had closed early. My mother knocked loudly on the door. There was no reply.

'I have to have white socks!' I insisted. 'The others have white socks.'

'Well, you're the one who hasn't, she said. 'The shop's shut.'

My mother went back to the mill. I went to the hall in Blakey Street.

Miss Wilkinson and Mrs. Williams were there already. The two other girls were there with their mothers. They both looked beautiful. Shirley had a long blonde plait down her back, with her blue ribbon plaited into it. Kathleen had dark brown ringlets, her ribbon pinned to one side.

Miss Wilkinson and the others looked down at my feet. I tried to explain what had happened, as my feet started to pinch in my small tight patent shoes. Miss Wilkinson had a word with Shirley's mother; then came back to me. She took me aside – 'Joyce,' she said, 'Shirley will go on stage and sing first, and you will now go on last. I have arranged with Shirley's mother, that when Shirley has sung, she will take off her white socks and lend them to you. I have to go now, and explain the change in the programme to the adjudicator.'

Shirley sang. A few moments later, her mother came and handed to me Shirley's white socks. She didn't speak, just half smiled. I took them and thanked her. They were far too big. I folded them under my toes, but that made my shoes tighter than ever.

I went on stage and sang 'The Apple Elf' and 'The Windmill.' I knew I'd sung the songs better than the others, by the applause. I got the highest marks, and we each got a certificate, that Miss Wilkinson had framed, and they were hung in the school corridor for all to see.

My grandma had written to the school to tell them about my change of circumstances. She stopped sending parcels to me, as by now I'd been sent all my clothes. She sent me a letter now and then, and put a 2/6d postal order in. She told me I could have Rosebud whenever I wanted her, but perhaps she would be safer staying where she was for now. I didn't want Rosebud to live at my mothers. I didn't want my sisters to have her and probably break her. I would leave her where she would be safe, and one day, I would give her to my own little girl.

Me, aged 5 or 6, with my Uncle Frank.

Grandma, Aunt Eva and friend June.

On the farm with great Aunt and cousin.

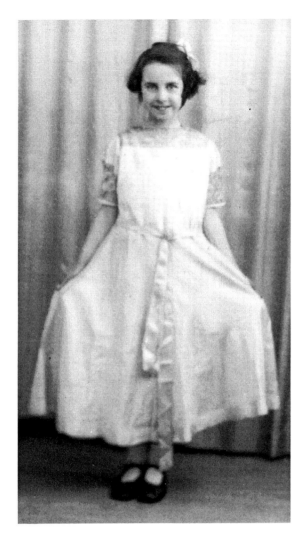

Dressing up, aged 9 years.

A serious 16 year old.

Student nurse.

## CHAPTER THIRTEEN

With others in my age group, I sat the eleven plus examination. No fuss was made about it at Blackamoor School. Children there had enough to worry about, and I think the teachers knew it.

I wrote a beautiful essay about the thoughts of a scarecrow as he stood in a lonely field, dressed in a red hat and scarf. The rest of the exam I don't remember – but I failed it anyway. That was a blessing in disguise. I would never have had the uniform, books, PE kit, and all the things I would have needed to attend the High School or the Technical College.

I was enjoying my school dinners more. I even ate the cheese pie, if I asked the dinner lady for a small helping. My main worry I had about them was not being able to pay for them.

The dinner money was 2/1d. It was collected by Miss Wilkinson on Monday mornings. Each class of pupils went in turn to wait outside of her office, and go in one by one to give her the money. She had a few a words with each of us, while she entered our name, to say we had paid, into a big red book.

Even though I asked my mother on Sundays for the dinner money, she somehow managed to forget to give it to me. When I heard the front door slam early on Monday morning, as she left home to go to the mill while we were still in bed, my heart would sink as I went downstairs to find she hadn't left my dinner money.

I made all sorts of excuses to Miss Wilkinson. I told her

I'd forgotten it, or, I'd lost it. Each week I had to think of something different to make up. If grandma sent me a postal order, I would pay with the money from that.

The dreadful thing was, just before we sat down to eat, in the long dining hall on Mondays, Miss Wilkinson read out of the big red book, the names of the children who had not brought their dinner money. I was so ashamed.

My dad came home in his 'borrowed' army truck more often, and told us the war would be over very soon. We were winning the war, and things would be back to normal soon. What was normal? My age group didn't know. Perhaps it would be like it was on the cinema screen. Perhaps like it was in America, where everyone seemed happy. My dad said we would have lots of fruit. The shops would be packed with food. We would be able to eat as many eggs as we liked, not one a week like we were rationed to now. He told us we would have radios with windows, where we could see the people telling stories. We would be able to see Dick Barton every night, like a cinema in our own house. It would show people dancing and singing. Our houses in the dark streets would be painted in all different colours, he told us.

I like my dad coming home, and telling us about all the wonderful things that were going to happen after the war. I did not like it so much when he argued with my mother though. Usually they argued about who had smoked the most Woodbines. Sometimes they argued when they came back at night from the pub. They used swear words, and spoke in loud voices, but he was never home for long, and I was always sorry when he went back.

The evenings were becoming lighter, and the women who

lived in the street, and who had been in the mill all day, came out of their homes after tea, to stand at their doors, taking the air, and chatting. They talked about money, men, new babies, who had them, and how not to have them. I sat on the doorstep listening in. It was in the middle of one of these chit chats, that my mother pointed at me, and told them, 'That one was conceived on the canal bank!' The women laughed. 'Oh! Annie!' said one. 'You must be special, Joyce,' said another to me.

I wasn't quite sure what conceived meant. I though it was something holy or religious. I remembered some words I had to recite when I went to Sunday School – 'He was 'conceived' by the Holy Ghost.' Was it something I'd done? Did it make me special? Should I become a nun?

I had visions of myself going into St.Alban's Catholic Church, and saying to the priest – ' Father,' I would say, 'I was conceived on the canal bank.' He would look stunned, as though a miracle had happened. He would put his hand on my head, and say some of those funny words in latin. 'My child,' he would say, 'you have to become a nun!' and the church bells would ring. He would gently lead me by the hand, and take me to the convent on Whalley New Road. I would leave Freme Street, and never go back. I would walk in the lovely gardens of the convent and talk to the birds. The women would stand at their doors, and say, 'Joyce went to be a nun. She was special.'

I told Letty! 'I think I might go to be a nun, and live in the convent.'

'You What!' she exploded. 'You are not even a catholic.'

'But my mother is, and anyway, I've found something out - it's special!'

'Go on – What?'

'I was conceived on the canal bank!'

'So What?' She wanted to know.

I had to confess that I didn't know what conceived meant. Letty soon put me right.

'It means that your dad was a randy sod,' she told me. 'I was conceived behind King George's Hall, after my mother had been to a dance there one Saturday night. A lot of people are conceived on the back row of the cinema. That's where they do 'thingy'. Dirty Buggers!'

I soon forgot all about being a nun!

Our new money making plan was taking shape. We chose the homes where they had a small baby. Letty knocked on one door, while I knocked on another. 'Would you like me to wheel your baby out?' we asked very politely. If the baby was already outside in its pram, it made it easy. 'Should I just wheel your baby up and down the street?' we asked. I would try to choose the baby who had the biggest pram. Manton, or Silver Cross, but most families had not got the money to buy prams like that. We wheeled the babies out together. The mothers would give us a threepenny bit or even a sixpence when we got back. Letty got bored. Babies were not her scene. My mother found out about my 'baby minding.' 'If you want to baby mind, there are two at home you can practice on,' she said. So that was the end of that, but at least I'd earned enough to pay off some of my dinner money that was owing.

School holidays were never a problem to my mother. While other women who worked in the mills took their young children to be minded at their grandmas, or to anyone who would have them – my mother had me! Nine long hours a day, I looked after my sisters. It wasn't one of my favourite pastimes by any means. Somewhere deep inside me was a maternal instinct, but not for my sisters. They invaded what little space I had. My books and all my belongings were kept in a cardboard box in the bedroom I shared with them. I really got mad with them if they touched that box.

Most days when I had them in my charge, I trailed them round the town, or into Corporation Park. They were too big to sit in a pram, but too small to walk very far. We had an old pram. It was used to collect coal in, from the colliery at the back of Harwood Street. Outside of the colliery gates were lumps of coal, dropped by the coalmen, as they loaded their carts and lorries. In the winter months my mother had sent me, with the other children in the street, to collect coal in the pram. It was not a pram to show off with. It was fawn coloured, or had been, medium sized, with no middle in it. The purpose being, that my two sisters could sit in – one by the hood, one by the pram handle, with their little legs placed in the gap in the middle. I hated that pram, but it was easier than walking with them.

It was so heavy, as I pushed it up Earl Street, along London Road; then the very steep Dukes Brow, leading to the park. With a bottle of water, and a pile of jam butties, we'd stay in the park all day.

Corporation Park was built in the early thirties, by the men of the town who were unemployed. The impressive front entrance was on Preston New Road, through the black wrought iron gates, bearing the coloured crest of the town, with words to match the effort of this amazing fete these men left as their legacy to the future generations – 'Arte et Labore.'

If I had taken the route through the town, to enter the park at the front, I still had the hill to climb with the pram, and was glad to rest in the delightful Remembrance Garden just inside of the gates. Two huge stone lion's heads dominated this tranquil setting as fountains of water gushed from their mouths, splashing onto the rose bushes around them. 'Can we see the lions being sick?' my sisters would ask.

Another statue, of 'Flora,' stared down at us as we made our way up to the pond, passing the abundance of coloured Rhododendrons. Then to the open field, where we would stay, drinking fresh water from the bubbly water fountain, sliding on the massive slippery stone, and if the weather was cold or wet, sheltering in the warm conservatory among the palms and exotic plants.

Letty invited me to a wedding!

'It's on Saturday morning at St. Alban's. It's to be a big do,' she told me. 'Wear your best frock. It was in the Blackburn Times – Alderman Somebody or other is marrying one of those nobs from up Wilpshire.'

'Do you know them.' I asked her.

'No! course not, But anybody is allowed to go into a church and watch a wedding – It's God's house! So are you coming?'

'Yes!' I said, as I always did to Letty.

I was really excited. To watch a proper wedding, just like on the films. Everybody wearing big hats and crying.

We waited outside of the church, watching the big black shiny Daimler cars roll up, and all kinds of beautifully dressed people getting out of them. They smiled and chatted to each other, speaking with nice voices. The photographer was taking photos, and asked Letty and me to get out of the way more than once. It wasn't a sunny day. It was cloudy and drizzling. I had my wellingtons on. I wore them a lot, as all my shoes were now too small.

It was time for the bride to appear. Letty said it was time for us to go into the church. We went in and sat on the back pew. It was magnificent in there. The lights sparkled, the flowers cast their scent, as they cascaded around the altar and the pulpit. The organ was playing, and the statue of Jesus looked down upon it all as he hung bleeding on his cross.

A young priest came up to us. His feet hardly made a sound on the red carpet that had been laid out for the bride. He whispered something to Letty. She shook her head. He was telling us to leave. We got up to go. 'You have no business here,' he said, as he quickly ushered us through the door.

'Yes we have,' shouted Letty. 'It's God's house!'

'Not this morning it isn't,' he answered.

'Anybody can go in church at anytime, and I'll tell the pope you said that.'

'Scram!' he told us.

We got outside just as the bride was walking up the path with her dad. She wasn't very pretty, and a bit old, but her dress was a silvery white, and her veil blew in the wind. Her photo was in the Blackburn Times the following week. I cut it out, and took it to school. ' I went to that wedding last week,' I told my friends.


'Lippy! – That's what you are getting,' my mother said to me. Too bloody lippy for your own good!'

On that Saturday morning, I hadn't done a thing right. I'd been a long time going to the shops. I'd bunked off to go to the wedding without telling her, and she'd had to go to Jennings for the pies and gravy for the dinner.

It was when she was settled in her chair with a newspaper over her head, which she did when she was having her catnap in the afternoons at weekends, that I asked her – 'Will you leave my dinner money for me on Monday?' She removed the newspaper. 'I thought you were going to take those two to the slipper baths,' she nodded towards my sisters.

'I am,' I said, 'but I'm just asking about my dinner money.'

'Then don't! I've given you the money for the baths, now get going,' She replaced the paper over her head. I felt brave all of a sudden, and asked her a question I had wanted to ask her for a long time – ' Mother – did you not want to have me?'

'What?'

'Did you not want to have me?' She didn't move.

'That's a laugh,' she said from behind the newspaper, 'I didn't want to have any of you. Now buzz off!'

'No, but mother, did you' …. I was cut short. The newspaper came from her head. 'Out! Get going! Sod off!'

'I bet the Queen doesn't swear at Margaret Rose,' I said, on my way out.

'I bet she doesn't,' she shouted after me, 'and I bet Margaret Rose isn't as lippy as you.'

I took my sisters to the slipper baths.

One thing in my mother's favour was that she always took us to the funfair when it came to the town. Usually at Easter time, we walked with her to the Market Square, that was taken over with swings and roundabouts, bumper cars, the waltzer, the big wheel, and stalls where you could win all kinds of prizes. The war had not stopped the joy of the funfair for the crowds that thronged there. I went on the caterpillar and the dragons, they being more tame than the other rides. She then took us into 'Sutcliffes' – a café, where we sat at the counter on high stools and ate a great plate of stew, with pickles and red cabbage.

I think, sometimes, she tried harder than I knew.

Ask no questions and you will be told no lies, I was often told. So, on the Monday morning, instead of going to school, we boarded a train at Preston, to travel to London; then on to a quaint little village called Danehill, near Haywards Heath – I asked no questions.

If it was, as I suspected, my dad had been 'up to his antics' again, and my mother was going to sort things out with him, I was not to know, and would not be told.

On that long journey I closed my eyes as the train took me further and further away from Blackburn. I did wonder what Miss Wilkinson would think when I didn't turn up at school, what Letty would think when she called for me, and I was gone. When would we go home again? I kept my eyes closed for most of the journey; then I wouldn't have to amuse my sisters. I imagined a fairy godmother coming to me. She would wave her wand, and say, 'You are going to the South. It is sunny there. The people talk funny, but they have gardens and bathrooms. There are trees in the streets. You will love it!'

We arrived eventually, in the blackout, at the small country village, and taken into a house to meet the parents and four children, who my mother seemed to know already.

Next morning in the light of day, I explored my new surroundings. The house, situated in the middle of the village, on the main road, was fairly big. It was quite old, and semi-detached. It had enough rooms to accommodate my mother and us three in the front bedroom. There was no bathroom, but had a large back garden, with a small orchard of apple trees at the far end. The only thing that spoiled it was the cess pit, that took up a large corner, and the tub toilet, that the man of the house emptied twice a week.

They were nice people. 'Uncle' was a baker, getting up very early in the morning to work in the village bakery, across the road from the house. He brought home warm bread and jam tarts every day. His wife, 'Auntie,' was due to have another baby any day, and the front room downstairs was equipped with white enamel bowls, towels and a crib, and all sorts of interesting things the midwife had left, to await the birth.

We soon mingled with the other children – three boys, and a small girl, all younger than me. Auntie was a kind woman. Plump, of course, with a red jolly face, domesticated and smiley. The fairy godmother would have been right, I loved the village. The treelined country roads, the small grocery shop, the little church at the top of the hill was like the ones found on top of wedding cakes.

I didn't see much of my mother. She disappeared in the front room with Auntie, where they talked for hours. I didn't listen in. I like the village too much, and went out when I could, across the road, to the green fields, to talk to the beautiful horses there. A little black cloud came over me, when we were told – 'You three will be going to school next week!'

We walked with the other children, down the country lane to the small stone built village school, snuggled among the trees by the woods.

I didn't do anything outstanding during the ten weeks we were there. I did not shine in English, nor did I sing. I was average in most subjects. I did eat my school dinners though, and joined the other pupils in the schoolyard with skipping ropes and bean bags, or went for a romp in the woods with them after dinner, until the school bell sounded calling us all back to class.

Auntie's baby had been safely born. The house was a hive of activity that I tried to keep out of. It was hard to think of the war going on outside of that idyllic setting, at the start of the beautiful summer.

Before the end of term, the headmaster had arranged a school outing. We were taken on a coach to Brighton. I saw the sea for the very first time. I thought to myself – one day I am going to live by the sea.

My grandma didn't know where I was. I knew my mother would not let me write to her if I asked. I dare not ask Auntie for an envelope and stamp. I tore a page out of a school exercise book, and wrote my letter on it. I folded it carefully, and put my grandma's address on the front; then stuck it down with the thick white gloy we used in class. I posted it without a stamp, in the little red postbox, that was attached to a tree in the village street. A few days later, to my surprise, and to my mother's surprise, as she didn't think anyone knew where we were, my grandma replied, sending me a stamped addressed envelope, and a three shilling postal order.

'Now I wonder how she knew?' asked my mother, looking at me knowingly.

As we ate our warm bread for breakfast, straight from the bakery, I was told by Auntie, that I would have to stay off school because my mother was not well. She was in bed, looking very white, and the doctor had been sent for. In less than an hour the ambulance had arrived. She was wrapped in blankets, and taken to the hospital at East Grinstead, a town quite a distance away.

'You will have to help to clear the bedroom,' said Auntie, 'I can't do it, with the baby to look after, and my husband should not be expected to.

Going in to the bedroom, I could not believe my young eyes at all the blood I saw. The bedding and sheets were soaked, the chamber pot was full, and a bucket half full by the side of the bed. I stripped the bed, rolling the blankets and sheets together, taking them downstairs where Auntie was going to wash them. Uncle came home from his second shift that morning at the bakery, and he and his wife had a long conversation in the front room. He went into the bedroom, and carried the chamber pot and bucket downstairs and into the garden. He took them up to the cess pit; then dug a hole in the ground. Auntie came to me – 'You will have to see to this, my love. Uncle can't face it.'

I was told to empty the chamber pot and bucket into the hole, and cover it over with soil. They went indoors.

I emptied the pot; then carefully tipped the bucket. Among the blood – was the body of a very small baby. It slithered out of the bucket and into the hole. At the bottom of the bucket, remained its tiny head. I had to shake the bucket to pour it out. It was all blue and red and jellified. I don't know what I felt. I was not afraid, or appalled, although I hated the sight before me. I covered it quickly with the soil, as I'd been told, and walked away.

Two weeks later, school had closed for the summer, my mother was discharged from the hospital, my dad had appeared on the scene, we'd said 'Goodbye' to the family and to the south, and travelled back to Freme Street.

My mother never spoke of the episode to me, nor I to her.

## CHAPTER FOURTEEN

Letty listened as I poured my heart out to her. It was as though we had never been to Danehill. The word was not mentioned in our house. Letty was the only one I could speak to about it. She had passed her eleven plus exam, and was going to the Technical College after the summer holidays. She showed to me her new uniform of cream and brown, her PE kit, white gym shoes, and hockey stick. Even though I was eleven years old, it had been decided by the doctors at the school clinic that I should remain at Blackamoor Open Air School.

Miss Wilkinson and the other teachers at school, along with Nurse Kelly, welcomed me back, but made little reference to my trip to the south. If they had contacted my mother about it, they kept it from me.

I was made a prefect and a house captain of Lister house. We had four houses dividing the school, with names of medical pioneers – Lister, Cavell, Nightingale, and Simpson. I played my role well, being capable of giving votes of thanks on behalf of the school to important visitors. Greeting parents politely when they attended speech day or other events, and keeping the younger pupils in order. One of my duties was to help Nurse Kelly with her morning surgery. Children stood in line outside of her small room, coming in one by one, to be attended to, and treated for various complaints. Boils, cuts, special medicines etc. I called the names of the children in turn, and helped to clear and tidy the surgery when they'd gone.

I was also a 'teacher's girl.' This meant leaving the class half an hour before lunch, to set up the staff room for the teachers to dine there. I laid the table with clean white napkins, and water in a special glass jug; then went to the kitchen to collect their meals in a small hot trolley, that I wheeled along the corridor back to the staff room, where I served them. Two of us were appointed to do this duty, and when we had served the staff, we were allowed to help ourselves to whatever food we like from the trolley, and eat it in a side room. There was always a choice, and the puddings were delicious.

The war being over meant little to me. I watched the rejoicing on the cinema screen, when I was allowed to go on Saturdays. The crowds surging round the palace gates, to see the Royal family on the balcony. The American soldiers kissing their new sweethearts for the last time, as they boarded the ships at our ports, to take them back home.

I sat at a trestle table that had been put up in the middle of the street, and ate jelly and custard, while I waved my paper union jack I'd been given at the street party with all the other children in the who lived there.

I was glad to see the blackouts taken down from the windows, and stood in wonder when the street lights were lit again. I didn't need to carry my gas mask to school any more. When asked to sing at school, I sang 'When The Lights Go On Again.' Mrs. Williams said I was just as good as Vera Lynn.

In my own small world – my clothes were becoming fewer, most of them handed down to my sisters, my shoes, becoming thinner on the soles, and let water in. My dinner money was still a constant worry. I dreaded having nits in my hair, and combed it with a steel comb every night. I hated sleeping with my sister, and I wondered why my mother was always saying she had no money, when she worked in the mill full time, and got an allowance for us from the army, as Letty had informed me. I did not complain, or ask for money, but still fiddled the change when I went to the shops. It was Letty who would give to me an old pair of socks, or a cast off cardigan without her mother knowing.

My mother and me did not have conversations. When she got home from the mill, tired, with cotton fluff covering her hair, and not much to look forward to, except another long day tomorrow, she was too 'done in' to bother with problems. She spoke to me when she had to, but I don't remember her ever touching me, not even to wash my hair, that I did myself.

But – never mind! My dad was coming home soon. He was to set up in business with my Uncle Frank. They were going to be the best Painters and Decorators in town. We were going to be rich, and have a big house with a bath, and a garden.

With a new grey suit, and a £100 allocated to him by the government, my dad, with thousands of others, duly became demobbed, coming home to 'a land fit for heroes' or so they thought. To welcome him home, I made a huge poster, with a picture of a warm fireplace, with slippers in the hearth. I hung it over our cold fireplace, where I could never get the fire going.

Things became better for a while when my dad came home. There was no mention of me going to live back with my grandma, nor did I expect there to be. That part of my life was long gone.

128

I got a bed of my very own. It wasn't new, and had a flock mattress that had to be shook and pummeled every day to get rid of the lumps, but it was mine! Someone had given it to my dad in exchange for him painting a ceiling. He got a lot of things for painting ceilings! We also had extra blankets that dad had acquired when he left the army. They were coarse and grey, but warm. He did not bring enough for us all to have one, but I was given his thick khaki army coat to put over me in bed.

He made a list of household jobs to be done. He hung the list on the wall by the sink. My jobs were cutting up newspapers into decent sized squares, and threading them on wool, to hang behind the lavatory door. Until then we'd just taken a piece of torn newspaper with us when needed. I still had to empty the chamber pot, but only from our room, my mother emptied theirs. Neither did I get out of lighting the fire when I got home from school, but he had got us a one bar electric fire we put on in a morning, before we went out in the cold. On the list he stated – we were not to use the electric iron to iron one item, like a blouse or a hair ribbon. Lights must be switched off when we left a room etc; etc.

He even put my mother's jobs on the list –

'Like Hell!' she told him.

He decided we should be given spending money. I was in heaven! He gave me ninepence on Fridays, and I got to go to the cinema with Letty on Saturdays. I had to take the money for the cinema out of my spending money, as dad said that was my choice, but I still had threepence left. Sometimes I saved it, sometimes I bought a mars bar. If I didn't go to the cinema, I bought a sixpenny saving stamp from the post office. That pleased my dad. 'You've got brains, kid,' he told me.

We did not see much of Alice, or Pauline and little Frank, my cousins. My dad didn't like Alice, so she kept away. But my lovely Uncle Frank was back!

I saw him nearly every day. He came on his motorbike. He looked a bit older, and had more meat on his bones, as my grandma would say, since I saw him last, but he still had that same lovely smile, and whistled 'When They Begin The Beguine' as he came up the backyard to the house.

Together, he and my dad discussed the cost of paint, customers who wanted their front rooms beautyfied, wages and expenses. They sat talking it out while they smoked like two factory chimneys. My dad had a wonderful idea. Wallpaper was scarce just after the war, so he emulsioned the walls with a cream or white emulsion paint; then rolled up a piece of cotton rag, dipped it in a strong solution of soot, taken from the chimney back, and water. He then 'rag rolled' it up the wall – where it produced a wonderful pattern, like a black palm leaf. He did it on the walls of our front parlour first. All the neighbours came in to see it, and loved it. Bookings for decorating flooded in.

I looked forward to my Uncle Frank coming, although he took little notice of me. He just said 'Hello love,' when he came in, and 'Bye love,' when he went out. I was just another niece. He never knew how much I loved him.

Over Christmas my dad had painted a huge Father Christmas on the bedroom wall, and bought me a brown wooden desk to put all my personal things in, so I could throw my box away that I kept under my bed.

He bought Scott's Emulsion that he made us take every morning – a thick creamy liquid, cod liver oil based tonic, that made what few spoons we had in the house smell and taste of fish.

He removed the sink, the tin boiler that we did the washing in, and the gas oven from out of the back living room, and built a shed in the back yard to house them.

We had fewer cockroaches when my dad came home from the army. Maybe they were scared of him. Before that, they were everywhere, even in the teapot. Every house had them in our street, although most of the women kept their homes as clean as new pins. Only one woman, a prim and proper type, no children, didn't bother with anybody, said she hadn't got them – until – Letty swept some up on a shovel, and put them through her letter box. 'She's got some now!' said Letty.

Everyone was friendly with everyone for a few months after the war. My grandma's brother, Henry, visited us, with his son, Derek. He was two years older than me. A quite lad, and a bit on the shy side. He taught me how to play Monopoly. We played for many hours over the New Year Holiday. They lived near, and Henry had helped my mother out during the time my dad was in the army. He moved her furniture on a lorry when she moved house. He was divorced, and sadly his daughter had died from diphtheria, making him warm to us three girls. He was a kind and caring man. Suddenly they stopped visiting us. I did not know my dad had accused him of sleeping with my mother while he was away. I didn't see them again. Like a lot of people in my life – they just went away.

I was sad to hear, many years later, when Derek was a young man, Henry had found him dead in bed one morning. He had died in a diabetic coma.

Letty and I were still confidantes. We met when we could,

after school, for a few minutes at least. Her parents were working, and we went into her house, where she poured out a huge helping of All Bran cereal into a bowl, smothered it with milk and sugar, and with two spoons we devoured it between us.

I had not seen much of her over the Christmas holiday, as my dad would not let any of our friends come into the house, and Letty's young and newly wed cousin had been staying with them. Letty wasn't pleased, as she'd had to sleep on the sofa downstairs, while they had occupied her single bed upstairs.

'They did 'thingy' in my bed,' she said. 'Doing bloody 'thingy' while I was freezing downstairs.'

'How did you know?' I asked.

'I could hear them!' Letty could be very descriptive. I was all ears, as she went on – 'It's a wonder the whole rotten street didn't hear them. She kept shouting, 'Comfort me! Comfort me!' I burst out laughing at this, and so did Letty. We threw ourselves about, laughing 'till we cried. We couldn't stop. For months we laughed about it. We only had to look at each other. Even in church, where we went sometimes to get out of the cold, Letty would mouth the words 'Comfort me!' and we would go into hysterics.

Miss Wilkinson took assembly, reading out school news and topics of interest to us. On that particular day, she concluded with – 'Now I have to read out the names of the pupils who will be well enough and strong enough to leave us at Easter, to attend other schools.' My name rang out from the list she was reading. The school doctor had decided at my last medical, that my health was so improved as to enable me to continue my education at Bangor Street Girl's Secondary

School.

So it was 'Goodbye' Blackamoor Open Air School.

I looked at it for the last time from the bus window. We had our school concert that afternoon, singing lustily 'I Vow To Thee My Country.' The leavers had shaken hands with the teachers and staff. I handed in my prefect and house captain badges, and gave a hug to my friends who where staying. I did not cry as I left, as some of the others did, yet I was sad. I knew I would never return, not even for a visit.

I put the thoughts and any worries I had about going to Bangor Street School to the back of my mind for the time being, as dad was taking us on holiday!

He took us to New Brighton, across the mersey, on a ferry boat, to a guest house, that had a bathroom, and a garden with greenhouses.

My mother had brought home some cotton material from the mill. A local dressmaker had dyed it – green for my sisters and a deep blue piece for me. She made us new dresses, even though there was only one each and we wore them all week. She had sewn a large white collar on mine that contrasted so beautifully against the blue. Even though it changed to a mottled colour the first time it was washed, I thought it was lovely. I had a pair of white and blue shoes with a small heel, my mother had got for herself from the market, but hadn't fit. With a small black handbag, also my mother's, I felt very grown up.

'Your girls are a credit to you, Annie,' the neighbours said.

As we set off, we looked like a happy family. My dad, handsome in his demob suit. My mother looking like a film star, her naturally dark curly hair hung about her shoulders. Her dark blue eyes fringed with the longest lashes. She never went short of new clothes, and had the figure to show them off.

At the breakfast table in the crowded dining room, where families like us were having their first post war holiday, spending dad's gratuity money, my mother said very little. My dad said a lot! He told the other guests what a wonderful big garden we had at home, what a big car he drove, what a splendid house we owned.

I felt very let down, ashamed and embarrassed. He started to go down in my estimation. The mirage I had built up of him while he was away all those years, started to fade. I loved him, but I was beginning not to like him.

My new navy blue gym slip and white blouse, bought from Tunstalls, was my uniform that I wore on my first morning at Bangor Street School. I looked smart, but I would have looked smarter still if I'd have worn black shoes. My shoes were brown lace ups. They were boy's shoes that someone had given my mother. I told my dad I had to have black shoes with my uniform. 'Don't let anybody in the world dictate what you have to wear,' he said. 'You be different!'

I didn't have a school tie, cardigan, cap, or blazer. I did not know where the thin washed out Gaberdine Mac, with a belt without a buckle had come from. Letty gave me her old school satchel. I was the new girl in a school of two hundred girls, streamed in to form 2A.

Out of school hours, jobs listed for me by my dad became ever increasing. On Thursday night I had to copy out his football coupon, while he took my mother to the Star cinema. They went on Tuesday night and Thursday night. Friday, Saturday and Sunday they went out to the local pub, or the 'Seventrees' Working Men's Club.

I hated doing those football coupons. I dreaded making a mistake, as I laboriously copied 1s 2s and Xs, with a fountain pen. He posted the coupon off to Littlewoods on his way to work on Friday morning, awaiting the big win of £25,000, that I knew we probably would not get, if I had copied the numbers wrong. Saturday, after my usual run of errands, he sent me to the Halifax Building Society on King William Street. He trusted me with his bank book, and the few pound notes he saved weekly for 'a rainy day'. This trip gave me the opportunity to while away some time in the public library. I always hoped to see my grandad in there, but never did. I spent time browsing through the books, enjoying the warmth and the quietness. My sisters went for the pies and gravy now, while I did other things. Yet, my mother always told me off when I got back for taking so long. 'There was a long queue in the bank,' I would say.

'I thought there would be! ' she would reply.

Letty decided we would start going to Sunday School! The Gospel Hall on Victoria Street. I could not believe my ears! Letty in Sunday School? I tried to reason it out with her. I did not like religion! OK, maybe I believed in a God I still said my prayers to every night, without anyone knowing, but Jesus – no fear!

She insisted – 'Don't be daft! They have the best parties at Christmas. We only have to go for six months and we get a prize. You can get out of doing the washing up after dinner, and we don't have to go straight home after. We can go up the park and stay out all afternoon.'

Put like that, and to go with Letty and have a laugh, did not sound so bad.

It was decided at home, I could go if I took my two

sisters. They took themselves after I had shown them the way, and Sunday offered to me a few more hours of freedom. We also went to the 'Bright Hour' on Monday evenings, where I was promised that Jesus would save me, and my life would be better. But he didn't, and it wasn't, so I stopped going.

While we were deciding what to do after a boring hour in Sunday School, apart from when Miss Sharrat the teacher, told us, 'Never do anything you would not like your mother to see you do,' and Letty and me nearly got sent out for giggling, Letty had one of her brilliant ideas – 'Let's go to see your grandma,' she suggested. The fear of God really went through me. My mother would kill me!

'Don't be so soft. Your mother won't find out.'

'What if we meet my dad on his way home from the pub? Where will we say we are going?' I put all kinds of excuses in the way, yet I wanted to see my grandma. I had never dared to think of going.

We walked through the backs of the streets, avoiding the main road. When we got to my grandma's back gate that seperated us from the backyard. Letty climbed the wall and looked over. 'I can see them in the living room,' she whispered. It was then that my grandma looked through the window, and spotted Letty on the wall. She came out into the yard, and shouted to her – 'Get down you little blighter! What do you think you are doing up there?'

'I've brought Joyce to see you,' Letty shouted back.

'You've What!' exclaimed my grandma. 'Good gracious me! Tom! Tom!' she shouted. I heard her climb the two steps up to the back gate, and unbolt the bar.

She opened the gate and I fell into her arms.

With Letty, I started to visit my grandparents nearly every

Sunday. It was the 'big secret.' My grandma knew it, and did not send me home with anything, apart from some spending money. I lied, and told her I was alright. I had everything I needed for school. I did not burden her with the fact I had only one school blouse, one pair of navy blue knickers, that I washed at weekend, while I wore a pair of my mother's. I had no vests or nighties. I had brown shoes, and only half a school uniform. My Grandad asked me what books I was reading. I mentioned the books we had at school. I did not tell him we had no books at home.

The visits continued, until one day, when I was feeling braver than usual, I asked my dad – 'Can I go to see my grandma sometime?' Although he did not see her himself, having been once as I knew of, since he left the army, he surprisingly said, 'Of course you can.' I was amazed! All that it took was to ask? Why did I not ask months ago? Then a fear gripped me. Did he know I was going there already? Would he use his belt on me for lying? Would he come up to me with his lip curling down, like he did to my mother when he got mad with her, and say to me - 'Listen! Don't try and kid one who's kidded thousands!' I was only learning that life with him would be a battle of wits. But this time luck was on my side. My mother chipped in 'You can go if you take the other two!'

I trailed my sisters with me for a few Sundays, but my grandma was not well, and it became too much for her to have four more persons to tea. My sisters had not the love for her I had, nor her for them, as they did not know each other. Eventually we stopped going, and from then I saw my grandma on occasions throughout her life.

At the time, I did not know I would be with her when she died, in her 72nd year. I would hold her hand as she passed away in her bed, in the front parlour, and as a trained nurse, I would administer her last dose of morphine, to ease her pain as she left the world.

# CHAPTER FIFTEEN

I realized if I asked dad for things, I would usually get what I asked for if it was reasonable. Asking him in front of my mother was impossible. The withering look she gave, meant I was in trouble. If I asked him for anything behind her back, and she found out, I was in deeper trouble. 'Big mouth! Have you been telling tales again? Always wanting, that's your trouble,' she would say.

So I did not tell him about my one pair of socks, and my brown shoes now had a hole in the sole. I stitched the socks up with white thread, and cut cardboard out of cereal boxes to put in my shoes. I held my feet in a certain way at school, so others would not notice the soles.

She did not think I needed anything, and he did not notice I hardly had anything. At night I slept in my only pair of navy blue knickers, and an old cardigan.

Summer months were easier. After a term at my new school, I took my first school report home, showing the results of not achieving much.

Good at English, was the opinion of the English mistress.

Bad at math's, the math's teacher Miss Heaps had written. Miss Heaps – a small thin woman, her peaky little face scrubbed clean, her sparse grey hair tied back into the smallest of buns. Dressed in her own self style uniform long brown dress, she stood at the classroom door as we silently filed in. Her usual greeting to us was to throw a piece of chalk into the air, catching it again, as one by one we passed her. She looked at each one of us without speaking, until I passed. Without reason, she would say in her stringy voice, 'Here comes the donkey!' Some of the girls would laugh, if only to please her, most stayed silent, joining me at playtime, to call her all the names under the sun. My secret wish, was – when I grew up and became a nurse, that's if I didn't become a famous actress, she would come into the hospital. I would be very sweet to her, and give her injections with the biggest needle I could find. I remained bad at arithmetic for always.

'Music – good! Sings well. True in tone. Not in the school choir, because she cannot stay behind after school hours to practice,' wrote the music teacher.

'Good at darning, but does not sew, because she does not bring the money needed for the materials,' stated the domestic science mistress.

'Good at Netball, and PE on the occasions she does it. She has no plimsoles, and has to borrow them. Shows no interest in Hockey at all,' was the message from the games mistress.

The games mistress failed to add – because when we go on the long walk to the hockey field, she is too cold to play the game when we get there, due to wearing the thinnest of Gaberdine macs, no vest, no cardigan, scarf or gloves, and wears shoes that leak. When she returns to school, she is almost collapsing due to the cold.

The headmistress summed up my report, by writing at the bottom

'Not allowed to go on the school outing to Whalley Abbey this year, due to not having the required uniform. Perhaps Joyce can make a better effort and show more interest next term.'

Seeing as I did not show the school report to my parents,

and signed it myself with my mother's name, it did not make a lot of difference, as I looked forward to the school holidays. Six weeks of freedom, when I could walk to Ribchester and Copster Green, to see the bluebells, golden buttercups, lambs, cows, and to feel the warm sun on my bones.

If I could get out of taking my sisters anywhere, I would, but they were close to each other and did not need me as much as time went on. The days I went with Letty, on the tram to Wilpshire, where I always sat on the left side by the window, to look out hoping to see my grandma in the garden, as we rode up Whalley New Road, were some of my happiest days. We got off the tram at the terminus and walked to Ribchester, to sit on the riverbank, making daisy chains, as we drank our Tizer, and ate our bread and jam. We then continued to the beautiful bluebell woods, to sit under the trees on the carpet of blue, or walk over the stone bridge into the old village, before climbing the steep hill back again to get the tramcar home.

Other times we took another route, walking through the fields to Copster Green, slightly afraid of the cows we passed, as they stared at us with ectopic eyes. The tea shop there was welcoming after our long trek, and we pooled what money we had, to sit at the tables in the garden, covered with red check cloths, and ordered tea and scones, leaving ourselves short for the tram fare back.

Cheekily, we still got on the tram at Wilpshire, even if we had no money at all. We went upstairs, sat at the front until we heard the conductor coming up to collect the fares; then moved to the back. When he got to us, Letty would pretend to look for the money in her bag, or her pockets, while the conductor patiently waited, and the tram continued on its way.

I then pretended to look for the money in my bag and pockets, until the conductor reasoned it out that neither of us had any money. By the time Letty had argued with him, we were at Bastwell, and nearly home when we were made to get off. If we recognised the conductor, and he recognised us before we got on the tram at Wilpshire, we would wait for the next tram.

If Letty had to go to Hockey, or to the swimming pool at Blakey Moor, to practice for the swimming gala, I would finish my errands and my jobs in the house, and sit in the sun on the doorstep, reading. My grandad had sent me a book for my birthday – 'Jane Eyre.' I read it over and over, until I almost knew every word. I knew it so well, I used phrases in my essays from it at school, that impressed the English teacher. I always finished my reading before my mother got home from the mill. If she caught me, she would say, 'Doing nothing as usual?'

During those lovely long holidays from school, I got my household chores done early; then went to the library, and on to the market for a big glass of sarsaparilla. If I'd managed to snaffle enough change from the errands, I'd walk through the Cathedral grounds on my way to the bus stop, and treat myself to the bus ride back to Freme Street. I lingered in the grounds, looking at the Cathedral. I didn't ever go in. If my fairy godmother had seen me there, she would have looked over my shoulder, and said, 'There is the Cathedral, my dear. One day, in the not so far distant future, you will be married there, in your white lace gown, with a flowing veil. You will marry a young man who you will have fallen hopelessly in love with. He will have dark wavy hair and the loveliest of smiles. Together you will have three beautiful children.' Her voice would drop a little, as she said, - 'but sadly my dear, it will not last. He will not love you as you will love him. You will lead an incredibly lonely life, but that will not stop you from doing all kinds of things…'.

It was only an 'if' and my fairy godmother did not look over my shoulder to tell me anything, as I walked down the Cathedral path, and got the bus home.

My Uncle Frank did not come to the house anymore. Him and dad had a 'bust up.' I had to listen while he poured out his bad opinions of my lovely Uncle. Things had gone wrong in the decorating business. One thing had led to another. Frank was accused by dad of draining petrol from his motorbike. I could not see that Frank would do such a thing, unless it was an emergency.

So, Frank joined the list of people who we didn't see. I only saw him once or twice in my life after that. He and Alice divorced. In his early fifties, my beloved Frank developed cancer of the throat. On the same day it was diagnosed, his 18 year old son was found dead, having taken a drug overdose, though not knowing of his father's condition. One year later my lovely Uncle Frank died.

One of the most horrific sounds heard in my life, was the sound of my dad hitting my mother.

On Saturday nights as they went out to the pub, I stood at the front door of the house, and watched them walk up the street looking like two film stars.

They returned about eleven thirty. I would hear them walking down the street, my mother's high heels clicking on the pavement, and the mumbling of their conversation as they opened the front door. Quietly at first, they argued and swore at each other. Then their voices became louder and louder, before the sharp slapping noises and the screams. Furniture and crockery fell over as she ran about the room. She shouted for us to help her – shouting my name first, then my sister's. I would tell my sisters to be quiet, to pretend we were asleep. She screamed 'God help me! God help me!' It went on for a long time, until he climbed the stairs, and fell into bed, sleeping soundly. She waited; then followed, whimpering, while her three little girls took their fingers from their ears, and got what little sleep they could.

I wondered what the neighbours thought of us. The people next door did not knock on the wall while it was going on, but they must have heard it all. Most of the people in the street now, just passed the time of the day with my parents, nothing more, apart from the women who felt sorry for my mother.

I dreaded to see her next morning. She would get up late, her lips cut, her face bruised. There would be a silence until he got up in the afternoon. If the row had not been so bad, he got up earlier, and went for a dinnertime drink.

We escaped to Sunday school!

The rest of the weekend, they talked about going to see a solicitor to end their marriage, but they never did. I hoped they would. I wanted them to part. I did not care if I went to live at the Cottage Homes, where my mother was always threatening to send us.

Sunday could be a day of hell!

If he went out, and came back in the middle of the afternoon, she would keep his meal in the oven. It was always dried up, but he always ate it. She threatened all day that she would never go out with him again, but if her face was not bruised, she would be ready at seven. Arm in arm, off they would go.

If he had made a real mess of her, she would stay in, even taking a day off from the mill on the Monday. He covered his embarrassment for his behaviour by being silly in front of us, as though nothing had happened. He'd say stupid things, like – 'Let's all watch your mother smile. Now watch carefully – there's a little smile coming, it's starting at the corner of her lips. Keep watching girls!' And my silly mother, among her cuts and bruises, would eventually try to smile. It made me sick to watch them.

Why could she not have handled him better when he was sober? Why would she never praise him when he decorated the house, mended things, and even made a small garden in the back yard? Why could she not bring herself to thank him when he gave her the wages every Friday night? I watched many times as he placed the money on the arm of her chair, and she did not even look up. He never had a day off work for any reason, although now he had gastric problems. She treated him disdainfully when he was sober. He took it out on her when he was drunk.

The historic villages and lush countryside that surrounded the dark smoky towns did not go unnoticed by the children in Lancashire. They escaped when they could, walking, or riding their bicycles for miles. Whalley, Clitheroe, Darwen Tower. Castles to see, green hills to climb, soft clear streams to dip your feet in, were not too far away. Nearer home, we walked to the 'Yellow Hills.' Hillocks covered with prickly but beautiful yellow flowering gorse bushes. If we went up out of the town, as far as Revidge Road, we could climb 'The Tank.' An erected stone square slab, at the top of a small flight of steps, where on a clear day, not only could you see across the town, but the eye could roam as far as Blackpool, taking in a glimpse of he sea.

On warm evenings, we went 'up fields' instead of congregating at the bottom of the street. The older children would call on each other during the day, or shout to each other while doing their errands – 'Are you going 'up fields' tonight?' We did not go in a crowd. We just knew we would see each other there.

We arrived at these fields by climbing the steep streets, Earl Street, or Calder Street, where pens, enclosing hens and goats, took place alongside rows of homegrown vegetables. Men to old to join the forces, had not only protected the homefront by firewatching, or being in the Home Guard, but had 'dug for victory' as well. They were proud of their produce, and spent many hours at their 'pens,' escaping their families, and putting the world to right, as they chatted and smoked their pipes.

These were the places Letty and me took to after Sunday School. First we walked along Randal Street, to a house where the man and his wife inside, made their own ice cream. It was so popular, the queue for it formed at their front door and down the street. Slowly we made our way into the house, through the living room, and out again through the back yard, having paid our two pennies, and collected a huge ice cream cornet, dripping with raspberry juice. There was no time to linger among the stainless steel bowls, whisks and bottles that filled their house.

While on a post Gospel Hall Sunday walk, Letty was in one of her playful moods, teasing and laughing –

'What's up with you?' I asked her.

'You know what's up with me!'

'What?'

'That lad who sits in the class opposite us at Sunday School, keeps looking at you.'

'Get away! Don't be daft!'

'And – you keep looking at him.'

'I Don't!'

'You do!'

I smiled, as she dug me in the arm. She was right, I did. There was no denying it. I did not think anyone had noticed, but Letty wasn't anyone.

Me and 'that lad' had been swapping glances for months, as we accidentally caught each others eye one Sunday, as we sat in different classes, in the same hall. He in the boy's group, me in the girl's, both pretending to listen, as the preacher told us how we could be saved – yet again.

When Letty said she was leaving Sunday School, I begged her not to. She told me during the next term, she would have far too much homework, hockey practice and piano lessons. But as a treat, we could both have a day off Sunday School the following week. Letty's dad had told her he would take us in his car to Lytham St Annes, the town near to Blackpool, with a sandy beach, and a big white windmill on the grass near to the sea.

After I'd asked my dad if I could go, and he had agreed, Letty and me talked about it all week. By Saturday we were in a real state of excitement.

On Saturday night, I let her into our house when my mother and dad had gone to the pub, and my sisters were in bed.

It was another of my jobs on Saturday night, to cook the small joint of meat my mother bought for the weekend. It was cooked on Saturday; then my dad could have a sandwich off it when they came back, and the rest was warmed up again for

147

the Sunday dinner. While the meat cooked, we finalised our plans for next day. What time Letty would call for me very early in the morning, how much money we could take, what we would do when we got there.

I took the cooked meat out of the oven. It smelled delicious.

'Should we have a sandwich?' suggested Letty. As a rule, I never touched the meat, but a small slither off the top wouldn't go amiss. So, Letty and me helped ourselves to a meat sandwich before she left.

I tried not to listen for my mother and dad coming in that night. For once though, they had come in quietly, and half asleep, I could just hear their mumblings – until – a great loud thumping noise brought me too with a jolt. I nearly jumped out of bed. My dad was banging on the uncarpeted stair with his fist, then shouting out my name. At first I did not answer, but the banging got louder.

'What?' I managed to reply.

'Have you eaten all the meat?'

'No! Letty and me only took a bit for a sandwich.' I dreaded him coming up stairs.

'I'll deal with you in the morning,' he told me.

Thank God! All went quiet again, apart from their mumbling. Next morning I would be up early, long before they got up, and anyway, he would have forgotten about the meat by then.

I was up early. It was a sunny warm day – perfect for the seaside.

I heard Letty's footsteps coming down the street, and opened the front door quietly, so as not to wake anyone.

'Are you ready?' she asked. I nodded – then whispered – 'Perhaps I'd better tell them I'm going, I don't want to get into trouble.'

I crept upstairs, and opened the front bedroom door, where my parents lay asleep.

'Dad!' I said, softly. 'Dad, I'm going now.'

There was a long pause, and just as I was going to repeat it, he answered -

'Where do you think you are going?'

'I'm going to St. Annes with Letty.'

'Are you?' he asked.

'Yes, I told you about it last week.'

'Did you?'

'Yes.'

'And when are you going?'

'Now. Letty's waiting for me.'

'Is she? Well, you go and tell Letty that you are not going anywhere.'

'But she's.....'

'I said tell Letty that you are not going anywhere,' he said slowly, deliberately and cruelly.

By this time, Letty's mum and dad had pulled up outside in the car. 'I can't go,' I told them. Letty was as crestfallen as me. She knew I could not argue with him. I told her about the meat. Her mother got out of the car, and put her arm about me. She knew what my dad was like, and did not want any dealings with him. 'Never mind love. We'll bring you something back.'

They drove away in the early morning sunshine. I went inside, got my book – 'Jane Eyre', and sat on the doorstep reading, until the rest of the street woke up.

He did not mention the meat when he got up. I waited all day for him to say something about it. He did not mention it that day, or ever again. He did not speak to me at all that day. Not one word.

He knew he had punished me.

## CHAPTER SIXTEEN

It was by listening in that I found out my mother was pregnant. There were no signs of an expected new baby in the house. No talk of a new baby, no clothes, pram, cot, - anything.

A baby! Oh No! Where would it sleep? Who would mind it when my mother went to work? When they went to the pub? Lots of questions arose in my mind on behalf of that baby. If a girl, she would share our unfurnished bedroom, with no heat, and cold linoleum on the floor. On Saturday nights she would lay in bed with her fingers in her ears, trying not to listen to her parents fighting. If a boy, he would be bullied by my dad, unprotected by my mother. He would not be clever at school, because he would not have the chance to be. I thought long and hard about that baby. In my prayers I spoke to God about it. 'Please God, don't let it live here, for so many reasons.'

On the afternoon I went down Freme Street, on my way home from school, and a neighbour stopped me to say, - 'Give your mother my best, Joyce – I hope she's alright. Sorry about your little brother – poor mite!' it was no big surprise. My mother had stayed off work that morning, but I hadn't known why. She had been in labour, taken to hospital, and had a stillborn birth.

When things got back to normal, and they started rowing again, I learned, that while my mother was recovering in hospital, my dad had walked up Whalley New Road, carrying my brother in a small white coffin, and had stopped in the Cemetery Arms pub on the way! So he said!

We didn't have birthday parties. People did not come into our house. So when Harold Green invited all the children in the street to his, I went, but reluctantly. Not from my own choosing, I found I did not mix well in a large crowd. I would never come to enjoy idle and polite chit chat, and I always looked over silly in a paper hat, whatever the colour. Letty and me arrived together. Harold was in the parlour with his parents, receiving his presents. I don't remember taking Harold a present, I probably didn't. His small comfortable home was packed with children. After we'd had the usual party fare, that adults think children enjoy – red jelly with evaporated milk, small cakes with pink iced tops and fizzy drinks, that made the boys see who could burp the loudest – we played games. That for me was the very worst time.

Harold's parents organised us. We had to stay in the back room or sit on the stairs, before we were called into the parlour one by one, to perform some silly act, while everyone laughed and cheered at their humiliation. I went last but found that was a mistake.

Harold's mother called me into the room, while the others smirked and silently waited for me to be the next laughing stock. Harold was seated on the edge of the polished gate legged table, with a huge gold paper crown on his head, and a red and yellow towel round his shoulders. I was told he was a great Sultan from the east, and everyone had to kneel before him, and greet him in his own language. The others crowded round me, as I knelt down on the floor before Harold, looking up at his thick grey socks and nobbly knees. His dad handed me a card with funny words written on. I had to read them out as I bowed my head –

'O, Wa – Ta na – Siam!'

Everybody shrieked with laughter. I couldn't see the joke.

'Do you know what you have just said?' they all chanted.

I didn't! I shook my head.

'You have just said, O, what an ass I am!' They laughed even more, it being an excuse for the boys to throw themselves around the floor and over the settee, until Mr. Green calmed them down.

The most popular game though, was being blindfolded, and having to dip your hand into a bowl of water, with sausages floating in it. The others watched, making rude noises, as though they were going to vomit. You felt sure you had put your hand into the jerry pot.

Everyone said it was a good party. Nobody wanted to leave. Harold's mum gave us all a piece of birthday cake to take home as we left her parlour, leaving behind, torn paper hats, spilled drinks, cake crumbs, and a smell of sweaty feet. Harold was a lucky lad.


On the Friday night Letty took me to my very first jumble sale, I had a wonderful time routing among the stalls in St Michael's Church Hall. I was delighted when I found a black winter coat. I tried it on, and it fit.

'How much is it?' I asked the woman behind the stall.

'It's ninepence, love,' she said. I had ninepence – my spending money! I bought it!

The next week, we went again, and this time, I bought a navy blue beret for tuppence. I knew I wouldn't be able to afford a school badge for it, so I had the brilliant idea that I would embroider a badge on it.

After I'd been to the Halifax Building Society for my dad,

I called at the market and bought two skeins of embroidery silk, red and gold. That weekend, I sat on the front doorstep and laboriously copied a badge I had borrowed, stitch by stitch on to my beret. I was getting nearer and nearer to having a school uniform – I thought!

Miss Ellis, the headmistress did not think so. I was still sent into form 3B to read a book, when the rest of the form went on a school outing.

Dad decided we would have weekly meetings at home, to discuss what was right and what was wrong in the house!

Seeing as he was the only one who spoke, it wasn't much of a meeting, on the few occasions we sat round him, until he forgot all about the idea.

He decided we would only eat brown bread. That ironing had only to be done once a week, and because his stomach was playing him up, I would do all the cooking for him! He was fed up with my mother's fatty meals she produced. He did not realize how envious I was of his 'rotten diet' as he called it. He was the only one in the house to ever have bacon. When he cut off the rind, I would eat it as I washed up the dishes, devouring the taste, and promising myself I would have bacon every day when I grew up. If he didn't have bacon and eggs, or sausage and tomato, I was sent to Jenning's confectioners for something other than what we were having.

'Go and get your dad a meat pie and a quarter of boiled ham,' my mother would say. That was his staple diet for most of his adult life. My dad must have eaten more meat pies and boiled ham than anyone else on earth. I thought he was lucky, as I watched him eat it, while we had fried bread or beans.

'And another thing,' – he said at one of the meetings – 'I don't want anymore cheese sandwiches putting up in my snap box.'

'You like cheese sandwiches!' my mother interrupted.

'Not the way you make them, and not every day. What do you think I am woman, a bloody mouse?' She didn't reply.

I felt sad to see her so demeaned at times. She was so obstinate and hostile to him. I wished she could have handled him better, like some of the film stars handled their men. Either charming them like Deanna Durbin, or being a tough cookie like Barbara Stanwyck, who my dad thought was lovely. My mother was just as beautiful when she was dressed up, as any of these women, and could have wrapped him round her little finger if she had known how. I hated to see her bullied.

I imagined her born into a rich family, wearing riding breeches and a crisp white blouse. She would have a horse with a silky brown coat, and ride him through the fields near Copster Green, her dark hair flowing behind her

I became more unpopular with my mother, and for a week or two, it was very stressful for both of us, as I cooked scrambled egg and such, while she stood by not saying anything.

Things got worse. After his dinnertime drinking sessions on Saturdays, dad would decide to talk to me at length, before he fell asleep. He talked about his girl friend Betty, who he met during the war. 'You would have liked Betty. You would have really got on together.' I squirmed, as I knew my mother was listening to it all in the next room.

The thing was to be out when he came in. As soon as I heard his motorbike coming through the back gate, I made a quick exit through the front door, either to go to the cinema with Letty, or anywhere to get out of the way.

'It's alright for you,' said my mother.

One Saturday I failed to escape. He came home from work really tanked up. Eventually he would sleep it off, and be ready to go out again at night. In between, he was a torment. He would dare you to do things!

This particular time, it was – 'Who is brave enough to come for a ride with me on the back of my motorbike?' We all went quiet. My mother shook her head to us behind his back. He went on and on, good humoured at first: then aggressive. Things were becoming uncomfortable – until I said, 'I am! I'll come with you on the back of your motorbike.'

You're bloody daft! He will kill you!' my mother said, as I followed him into the back yard, getting on to the pillion of his bike, without helmet or protective clothing.

He nearly did kill us as he bombed up Whalley New road to Wilpshire, and down the steep hill to Ribchester. He drove like the wind. My hands froze into numbness as I gripped him round the waist for dear life.

All of a sudden, we slowed down. The bike coughed and spluttered: then stopped. It had broken down! God had been watching over us! In the middle of a country lane – we had broken down! The bike had to be left there.

By the time we walked to the nearest tram stop, and got home, much later – my dad had sobered up.

Nothing would keep him from his work. So I knew it must be serious when dad stayed in bed, and turned a golden yellow colour. So serious, that he was taken to the Royal Infirmary for a 'partial gastrectomy' operation, that I'd looked up in one of my books.

While he was away, my sister's single bed was brought

downstairs, and put into the front parlour for his return, while she moved into the front bedroom to sleep with my mother.

My heart went out to him when he came home. He was so thin and yellow looking. He was too weak to stand properly, and had to be helped to wash. His legs would not take him out to the toilet. He suffered the indignity of having to use a chamber pot. This was not like my dad. All the bravado gone. I helped as best I could, before going to school in the morning. I gave him toast and tea, a bowl of warm water to wash, as best he could. I emptied the chamber pot, and banked up the fire, arriving at school just in time for assembly.

Miss Holgate, my form mistress and music teacher, had the job of inspecting our shoes as we sang the morning hymn, and recited the Lord's prayer. It was at that time, on the morning when I'd arrived at the last minute, that she tapped me on my shoulder – 'Your shoes are dirty!' she said.

'I hadn't time to clean them Miss. My dad is ill,' I answered.

'Well go home and clean them now,' she ordered. I left the hall in the middle of the last verse of the hymn, while teachers and pupils watched me go. It was a good thing Miss Holgate hadn't seen the soles of my shoes, and the Kellog's Corn Flake packet inside of them.

I spun out the time, as long as I possibly could, before going back into the class. I made dad a cup of coffee, and told him I'd gone back home because I'd forgotten something. I walked as slowly as I could, back up the hill, into the school gates, and into class. The register had been called, as I took my place at my desk. Miss Holgate closed the register, and looked up. In the awkward silence, she pointed at me – 'What have you got to say for yourself?' she asked. I stood up, and gripped the underside of the wooden desk in front of me. In my best voice, I said – 'I have never been so humiliated in all my life. I had a good reason why I did not clean my shoes. My father is very ill. I had to give him breakfast, help him to wash, and empty the chamber pot, as well as seeing my two sisters off to school.' Miss Holgate went a purply red. All I could concentrate on for the next few moments was a great blue vein throbbing on the side of her neck.

'Sit down!' she said firmly.

I liked Miss Holgate. She taught me a lot about music, but that was one time when I felt I'd been treated unfairly. I became good at sticking up for myself.

Because dad was too weak to argue, and my mother too tired, but mainly because they were off the booze, things were pretty quiet at home. The main concern was money. Although she worked full time, and although he couldn't go to the pub, or smoke since he was ill, they talked about money and the lack of it all the time. I could never see why we were so poor. Yet dad was worried.

My grandma had passed on to her eldest son many good traits that outweighed his bad ones he'd inherited from somewhere. Not only was he proud and independent, as clean as a new pin, and underneath, as soft as a puppy dog, but when push came to shove, he could turn his hand to anything, and hadn't a lazy bone in his body.

As soon as he started to make a recovery, he got my mother to 'acquire' some bobbins of coloured silk from the mill. He made a frame out of ply wood and tacks, and began making silk mats to put on tables, sideboards, and dressing tables for people who had them. Those mats were beautiful! In the softest of blues, pinks, lavender, delicate greens, and creamiest whites, fringed round the edges. He sat all day making the mats, while I sat half the night, making the fringes.

I held down a mat with my left hand, while I combed the silk out briskly with a small wire brush, taking care not to pull the strands. My mother took them to the mill to sell to her friends. The orders came in fast, until the overseer in the winding shed noticed a shortage of silk pirns. 'You'd better pack it in,' said my mother. 'You're going to have us behind bars.'

Then dad invented new ideas. Kiddy Cars came next. These were small wooden bucket prams, with two wheels and one long handle. Besides these, he made toy ducks that flapped their wings. He painted them bright yellow, finishing them off with cute faces with big eyes. Little tots walked along the range, pulling behind them toy ducks my dad had made. I was so proud of him.

On the day the doctor told him he would be alright if he kept on a gastric diet, took his stomach medicine, and laid off the alcohol, he cleaned down his motorbike, and went back to his decorating business.

Dad's stomach medicine had to be collected once a week from the surgery. Dr. Mallick was the only black doctor in Blackburn. I think he was the only black man in Blackburn. People thought he was wonderful! A big man with tight black curly hair, surrounding his cheerful face. His white teeth lit up his smile. His deep voice was reassuring. Even though I went straight after tea, getting out of doing the washing up, I still wouldn't get back until nine-o-clock, a bit later if I'd bought myself some chips on the way. His surgery was a small back room at the back of his house, in St. John's Street, in the shadow of St. John's Church. A queue formed outside of his back door, down the yard, and out of the back gate into the street. In all kinds of weather, his patients waited, filing slowly in to the house for their turn to enter the little room, with the plaque on the door, saying 'Surgery.' He was thought to have magic powers brought from distant lands. He made up his own medicines while you waited. . The women advised each other - 'Go and get a bottle off Dr. Mallick, Annie,' my mother was told when she was complaining how tired she was.

With the help of Dr. Mallick's magic potions, dad had got stronger. He was happy to be back at work. That meant we were all happy – until he started drinking again!

Letty couldn't come with me on the evenings I went to Dr. Mallick's.

Now in her fourth year at the Technical College, she had so much homework to get through. But on Tuesdays we met up to go together, and went arm in arm to the local newsagent, catching up on the news that was of interest to girls of our age. I'd missed her after she'd left Sunday School. I promised I would ask the superintendent if she could come to the Christmas party.

The local newsagent ran a small lending library. For tuppence, you could change your library book there. Letty chose a book about cowboys for her dad and a love story for her mother. If they had done or said something to annoy her, she chose books she knew they would not like. I chose a gangster book for my dad, and bought his five Woodbines at the same time. I was always careful to give him the right change out of the money he gave me for the errands. He was sharper than my mother. I didn't choose a book for her. She said she had no time to sit around reading books, apart from her magazine, 'Red Letter'. If we had any money, Letty and me shared it between us, and lingered on the way home, buying a penny bag of parched peas, or a stick of licorice root.

Sometimes by mistake, I chose a book my dad had already read.

'Oh, Kid! I've read this. Nip back and get us another,' he'd say, and I would have to trail all the way down the range again.

## CHAPTER SEVENTEEN

'Can I learn the piano?' I asked my mother

'What do you want to learn the piano for?' was her answer.

'Because Letty does.'

'Well, that doesn't mean you have to.'

I dropped the subject, not knowing that my dad was listening.

A week later, when I got home from school, sitting in our back living room, taking up most of the space, was a big iron framed piano.

My mother told me, 'Your dad got it for painting a ceiling. But don't think you are going to have piano lessons. You wouldn't stick at it and we're not throwing money away.'

'It's alright,' I explained. 'Letty said when she's been for her lesson, she will tell me all that her teacher told her, and how to play, and I can borrow her music books.'

'Did she now?' said my mother.

I'm not sure if the piano came from the back room of a pub, or not. It was very honky tonk, with one or two notes missing. I didn't care. I was going to learn how to play the piano. Not only would I be able to sing if ever I became a famous actress, I would be able to play as well.

The following Sunday, while we were out at Sunday School, my dad chopped the piano up in the backyard. We used it for firewood.

Nothing more was said.

Miss Ellis, the headmistress at Bangor St. Girl's School, was small and petite. Her brown hair combed into a neat roll all the way round her head. She wore thick rimmed spectacles, complimenting her green suit, and sensible shoes. I respected Miss Ellis, and always felt guilty eating chips in the street, when she'd told us streets were not for eating in. She told the girls, not to do everything there was to do before we reached the age of twenty one, or there would be no excitement left in life. I admired her for speaking out about the bible, telling us half of the stories written in it were not true, but there to illustrate a point. I felt sorry when parents sent nasty letters to her about her comments, and I verbally sprung to her defence when I heard girls saying, 'Miss Ellis does not believe in Jesus, and she should not be a teacher.'

On the morning she announced in assembly – 'Sir Thomas Beecham, the well known conductor, is coming to Blackburn next month, and Miss Holgate has given me a list of names of the girls she has chosen to attend the concert at King George's Hall to sell programmes, I could not believe my ears when she read out my name with the others. Miss Holgate had chosen me!

She knew I loved the music I was being introduced to in her lessons. Although she was less impressed when she heard me mimicking Kathleen Ferrier, but I heard she'd admitted to the other staff, that I could sing 'Blow the Wind Southerly' nearly as well as Kathleen herself. I was sorry I didn't like the voice of Miss Ferrier, who lived in Blackburn, had been a pupil at the High School, and who Miss Holgate adored.

Two weeks before the concert, Miss Ellis took me aside – 'You really must have the proper school uniform, Joyce, or

I'm afraid you can't go,' she told me.

I borrowed a white blouse and a tie from a girl called Marion. I borrowed a navy blue cardigan and a school beret from another girl called Joan. I polished my black shoes that I'd recently bought from the jumble sale, until they shone. I saved two weeks spending money, and juggled my mother's change from the shopping, managing to buy a pair of white socks from Tunstall's shop.

On the big day, Miss Holgate gave each of us a special yellow braid belt, to tie round our gymslips. As a treat we were given tea and cakes in the cookery room, by Miss Smith, the domestic science teacher. We then made our way, on the bus, to King George's Hall. Arriving in good time, we were shown the hall, and where to stand to sell our programmes.

It was one night, the first of many, when I took Letty's advice. I thought of home – the fire to be lit, the errands to be done, and I said to myself, 'Sod the fire! Let them light it, and sod the errands! Let them go for their own bloody milk and Woodbines.'

I had a wonderful time. The orchestra played 'Fingal's Cave. Miss Holgate beamed. She was so happy – and so was I.

The only thing that was ever shared between my parents, was the evening newspaper. Over their tea, they split the paper in half, my dad read the sports and horse racing results, whilst my mother read the births, marriages, and deaths pages. Without taking her eyes from her half of the paper, she said, 'Kings dead!' Without looking up from his half of the paper, my dad answered, 'It wasn't on the news.'

'Not that King! King who lives in the next street. He used to work at Birtwhistles.' He doesn't now, I thought to myself, as thoughts of having a day off school for a state occasion were quickly dashed.

O' him?' My dad nodded. 'He was a good worker was King.'

'Good at a lot of things from what I heard about him.' My mother smirked. 'I think I'll go round later, to pay my respects like. I've always wanted to see what they have in their house.' She looked across at me: then at my sisters, saying, 'See that these two get washed, and you can come with me.'

It was Tuesday, and I'd arranged to meet Letty. 'Don't you want your library books changing, dad?' I asked hopefully. He was still checking his horses. 'It'll wait,' he said. So I had to go.

My mother changed out of her clogs, and put some lipstick on. 'Can I put some lipstick on,' I dared to ask.

'What do you want lipstick on for?'

'Well, all the girls in our class put lipstick on.'

'Well, you're the one who doesn't. I don't think a dead fella is going to bother whether you have lipstick on or not.' She paused, before she added 'but knowing King, you never know!'

We walked round the corner into the next street. Mrs. King was on her knees, scrubbing her front doorstep. She had on a black pinny, and a flowery patterned turban, covering a head full of silver steel curling pins.

'Hello Cissie! We've come to pay our respects,' my mother said.

'Come in Annie. Mind me step,' Cissie whispered. We followed her in. 'He's in there. In't parlour, with his sister.' We walked into the parlour, to see the coffin placed alongside the fireplace, as that seemed to be the place where folks were placed when they'd died. His sister was standing by it. The orange curtains were drawn across the front window, bathing everything in a cosy glow. The coffin was reflected in the large mirror on the sideboard, making it look as though there were two dead bodies in the room. My mother said later, that his sister looked worse than he did, and she was right.

This frail little waif of a woman indicated to us to go to the coffin to see him. Mrs. King passed through the room with her bucket and scrubbing brush, on her way to the kitchen, without speaking.

There Mr. King lay, dressed to kill, in a tight fitting black suit, with his Billy Cock laid across his feet. His sister patted his moustache with the back of her fingers; then looked up at us. My mother nodded, so I nodded. Bending towards the sister, she asked, 'Did he have a stroke?' She mouthed the words without sound, as though he might hear. His mouth was slightly askew, I noticed, when I could bring myself to look closer.

'No,' his sister told us. 'He was eating a bit of treacle toffee when he died, so we left it, like.'

I think my mother had noticed before me, that his flies were undone. She leaned forward and said something I didn't catch, to his sister.

She shook her little head, overcome with grief for her brother. 'I know,' she spluttered. 'It is a bit small. It's his wedding suit. It's from his first marriage, not to this one.' She pointed with her thumb to the kitchen. 'Anyway, nobody is going to see his flies when the coffin lid is screwed on.'

On Saturday morning, Mr. King was buried. The women of the streets closed their front curtains, and gathered together on the corner of the street where he'd lived, to watch the coffin go by, and to see if the flowers they'd collected for, were in the hearse.

'He was a bit of alright, he was,' said one woman, smiling to the others.

'I heard he's being buried with his first wife, said another.

'If he is, I hope she bites his bloody arse!' said the first woman.

On the day Prince Charles was born, I stood in the Gospel Hall on Victoria Street, and prayed with the other Sunday School children for a happy and glorious life for him, while I occasionally glanced across the hall, to look at 'that lad' who had been glancing at me for the past year.

He had started to come to Sunday school on his bike, and was always the first to leave. As the Amens were being said, he would leave the hall, giving me a look as he went out. My heart sank a bit as I watched him go. I'd waited all week to see him. I'd even put two of my mother's metal curling pins in my hair on Saturday, and endured the pain of them all night. I made a special effort as best I could, with what I had, to look nice for him on Sundays.

Now Letty did not come to Sunday School, there was nothing to do but to go home after the service. I went the longest way I could find, or walked round the town looking in the shop windows, so as to be out of the house when my dad got home from the pub. For weeks after Sunday School, I'd been walking about on my own, going nowhere, getting colder and colder as the wintry days closed in, and for weeks 'that lad' had been passing me on his bike. He never spoke to me. He rode by, usually at the speed of sound. He was a show off! Good looking, dark hair slicked back. He had the darkest eyes, and brows, and a generous mouth with lovely teeth.

I left the Gospel hall on that cold grey November afternoon, to walk up Randal Street, onto Larkhill: then down

Brookhouse Lane and home. He rode past me on his bike as usual: then back again. He slowed up, riding by my side. 'Do you want to go for a walk?' he asked me. It was the first time he'd ever spoken to me. It must have taken a lot of guts for him to do that.

I don't know what I answered, but I do know he stopped coming to Sunday School on his bike. He still left during the Amens – to meet me – round the corner, and to take me on the longest walks of my life. We would go over the Yellow Hills, up Queen's Park, over Revidge, round Pleasington, anywhere to get out of the town, before we left each other, a few streets away from Freme Street, to meet again next Sunday. I adored him! He became my boyfriend, true friend, and confidante.

Going out at night didn't enter my mind at that age. My time at night was taken up. By the time I'd got through the errands and chores, and washed my one and only blouse, for school next day – it was bedtime.

The blouse never dried, and I had to put it in the gas oven next morning, to try to dry it off, but nearly always, I went to school with the collar and cuffs still wet.

My boyfriend was 16yrs old, and an apprentice motor mechanic. One of four children, his mother widowed, and a staunch church goer. He lived only a few streets away, yet it was difficult for us to meet other than on Sundays.

Letty came to the rescue! She decided she would leave me on Tuesdays when we got to the newsagents to change the library books. We wouldn't hang around and go to the toffee shop. I could meet my boyfriend instead. So, on Tuesdays he waited for me outside of the newsagents, on his bike, whatever the weather. I got home ever so late.

'Where the hell have you been?' was what I expected, and got, from my mother. The excuses came easily nowadays. 'There was a long queue, (that was my favourite one) The shopkeeper had some new books, but he had to unpack them. Somebody nicked something, and the shopkeeper had to run after him. I didn't care what I said, as I got told off, as long as I could see my lovely boyfriend.

With the bit of money I could accumulate during the week, I spent on clothes from the Friday jumble sale. Grandma didn't send me postal orders anymore, it would not have been fair on my sisters, but dad gave me a penny every time I made him a cup of tea, so that helped. I'd stopped going to the slipper baths, and washed myself down in the sink, instead. I stopped going to the Saturday afternoon cinema. That now, was only for kids. I bought clothes from the jumble that were far too old for me, trying to make myself look nice for Sundays.

I dreaded Christmas's at home. The silence on Christmas Day as my mother bathed her bruised face and arms. Dad stayed in bed for most of the day, sleeping off the fighting and rowing, and the guilt of the night before. We three girls opened what presents we'd got, pretending everything was alright.

When Letty and me got a chance to be together on the cold evenings, we would visit different churches in the district. If there was a Carol Service, we would sit at the back near the warm radiators. We pretended to sing the carols, making up different words – 'We Three Kings of Orient Are' - 'one in a taxi and one in a car.' If we managed to stay to the end, we helped ourselves to a mince pie and a cup of tea with the rest of the congregation.

I was looking forward to the party at the Gospel hall that year. Letty and my boyfriend would be there. I was chosen to read from the bible. I had rehearsed, 'And His Name Shall Be Called – 'Wonderful – Councilor – Lord of Lord's – King of King's' until I knew it well, and could render it in a strong voice. My mother said I could wear her red frock, with short sleeves and sequins sewn across the bodice. On the day, I curled my hair and put on the summer frock, making myself look about ten years older. It was too long, and I was freezing in it, as I had nothing underneath, apart from my navy blue school knickers. It was a rainy day. My mother would not let me wear her flimsy best shoes, so it was school shoes or wellingtons. I chose wellingtons.

With Letty, I joined in the childish games that I hated, keeping a lookout for my boyfriend. The hall was full of people. Soon it was time to read my piece. I went up on the stage and into the pulpit. I scanned the heads of the congregation, looking for him. I rendered the religious reading I'd rehearsed over and over again, just for his ears, with satisfaction to all. But – he wasn't there. I was so hurt.

On the following Tuesday when we met, he laughed when I told him.

Sunday Schools and their parties were not for him anymore.

When I asked dad if I could have a bike, I meant one like my boyfriend's, a racer with drop handles. When he acquired one for me (for painting a ceiling) a black sit up and beg type, without gears, I wasn't impressed, but as my grandma would have said – beggars can't be choosers. I learned, very quickly to ride it.

My sister wanted to learn to ride. If I was in a good mood, I would take her to the bottom of the street, and if the gang who hung around there were not about, to laugh and shout rude things – like 'get off and milk it' I'd sit her on the seat, and wheel the bike along, even though her short legs did not quite reach the pedals.

It was while we were doing this, that suddenly, out of nowhere, a voice behind me said, 'Can she not ride it yet?' I half turned – The next half hour became for me and my young sister a memory we would never forget. This creep of a man, thin faced, dressed in a long grey mac, grabbed me under the arms from the back, and dragged me up the slippery cobbles, with my heels scraping the floor, past the back gates of the terraced houses. My sister fell off the bike and screamed at the top of her voice. I screamed as well, and with that he let me go. I did not look back at him. Thinking he was running after me, I screamed at my sister to 'run'. I caught her up, and together we ran, leaving the bike with the wheels spinning round. The neighbours were standing at their doors. They shouted to us –'What's up? What's up, love?' Our front door was closed. We hammered on it until dad opened it. I blurted out what had happened as we stumbled inside. He shut the door on the prying eyes. He came towards us, and lifting his hand, he gave us both a stinging great slap on the face. We reeled back, stunned and in shock, but we knew not to make another sound. He and my mother were in the middle of tarting themselves up to go to the pub. They continued to get ready, as me and my sister sat in silence on the settee in the front room. Later, dad went down the street to recover the bike. His face was set. His mouth was tight.

171

The neighbours did not ask him what happened, or if we were alright. They went indoors.

'Don't ever, ever dare to show me up again like that,' he told us, as we sat together looking like two little ghosts. He accused me of 'playing with the fellas!'

They went to the pub as usual. I locked all the doors in the house behind them. Next morning I found a half crown piece in my pocket. I was never sure who had put it there! I didn't tell dad about it.

The following week while they were out, the same man walked up the street and past our front room window. I saw him from inside. I was petrified. I thought he was looking for me. I went to tell a neighbour across the street, and they took me in their house and calmed me down, before taking me back home, where my sisters were in bed, all alone. They made sure we were safely locked in, and when I begged them not to tell my dad, they reluctantly promised they wouldn't.

The episode, like so many in our home, had not to be mentioned. I didn't see the man again, but it left me nervous for many months after.

It left me cold, when Letty enthused about her sports day, hockey matches and swimming galas. I still didn't have any pumps of my own for PE. I couldn't find any in the jumble sale. A kind girl, in the next form always lent me hers.

I detested the days when my class filed in twos and walked down the range to the Blakey Moor Swimming Baths. Of course, I hadn't got a swimsuit, or swimming cap. When we got inside the doors, we were greeted by the attendant, who shouted to us –'Those with swimming costumes and towels, continue to the changing rooms. Those without wait here.' A small group of us waited. She then brought a pile of swimsuits, and handed them out to us. They were made out of cotton material with washed out stripes running through. Holes for arms and legs and a drawstring round the neck. Swimming caps were stored in a box. With luck, we found one that fit. A small whitish towel, was provided with the swimsuit.

I looked a freak in those suits, and resented the two pennies I had to pay to borrow it, usually out of my spending money. The pool was always packed with pupils from the surrounding schools. The water was cold and stung my eyes.

Miss Hodson, a huge lady, in a huge black swimsuit, instructed us in a huge voice. She made me stand in the water and hold the rail at the side, while she worked my little legs about, 'till I thought they were going to leave their sockets. Above the noise and commotion in the pool, she shouted to me – 'Pretend you are a frog! Pretend you are a frog!' I knew I would never learn to swim, but wished I could when I went to the cinema to watch Esther Williams. Her skin didn't go all goose pimply, and her eyes go all red with the chlorine. Her swimsuits were gorgeous!

The long walk back to school with my hair wet, and my skin damp, made me miserable for the rest of the day. I was glad to eat the hot school dinner when we got back, whatever it was. Some of the girls bought hot meat pies on the way, but I could never afford them.

One of the girls in my form never went in the swimming pool. The rumour got around that there was something wrong with her. Rumours soon got around in 4A. A quiet girl, prim and tidy. Tight short curly hair, her uniform beautifully pressed. She was no trouble to the teachers. Did her homework on time – but never went into the swimming pool. There's something wrong with her 'down there' was the whisper.

I asked her one day, 'Have you had an operation or something, that means you don't swim?' She knew I hated the swimming lesson, I made no secret of it, but was surprised when she confided in me.

'I don't like the water. I can't stand getting my hair wet Every body has a wee in the pool. My mother says the water must be filthy. So I tell the attendant every week, that I am having my period, and she sends me to sit in the spectators seats to watch.'

'Every week?' I asked her. 'Every week! Does she not twig it?'

'There are so many of us, she doesn't know one from another.'

'Have you started your periods?' I asked.

'No, not yet. Don't tell on me! Promise?'

I promised! But thought it was a tactic I would try for myself.

The next week, I stood in the queue for our revolting swimsuits. When it was my turn, I told the attendant, stating firmly – 'I'm menstruating!' I knew the proper name for periods. I'd learned it from a book I had got from the jumble sale. She must have known the proper name as well, as she sent me to sit in the spectator's seats. I joined the other girl, laughing and telling jokes, while the others pretended they were frogs and got freezing cold.

The girls in the class found out about my lie.

'You told a lie,' they said. 'You haven't even started yet!'

'I have!' I said defiantly. 'So shut up!'

They told the PE mistress. She questioned me about it. I put on my sincere face, and told her I was telling the truth. I had to keep up the charade for nearly a year, but it was worth it.

My mother got to know about my boyfriend. My sisters had told on me, when they saw me leave the Gospel Hall and go to meet him on Sundays, instead of going home. When she asked me about him, I denied it all.

'You want to be careful, Lady! You'll be finding yourself in trouble,' was the only comment she made.

I saw him as often as I could. I got in later and later from our walks, sometimes after tea, when they were getting ready to go to the pub, and my sisters needed organizing to get themselves to bed. Sunday followed its miserable routine at home. The previous day, mother scrubbed dad's white overalls, ready for him to wear on Monday. All day Sunday they were placed over a chair in front of the living room fire, hopefully drying. If they weren't dry by Sunday night, it was my job to iron them dry. I did this nearly every week, along with my white school blouse, while I listened to the Palm Court Orchestra on the radio.

As I hurried home from the chip shop, trying not to eat any, and hoping they would still be hot when I got there, so I wouldn't get told off, a lad out of Ice Street stopped me. 'Give us a chip,' he demanded. I took the newspaper off the top of the dish, and he put in his dirty big paw. This happened frequently if the lads round our end saw you with chips. It was better to let them have one, than to argue, and risk them taking half of them. He swallowed the hot chip: then spoke – 'I see that lad you know is doing something bloody daft for a bet on Friday night.'

'I don't know any lad!' I said.

'Come off it! Any way, if you want to watch him break his neck, he's going to ride his bike between two bricks on Bangor Street. Silly bugger!' He walked away.

Perhaps it wasn't my boyfriend he was talking about. But it was! Letty and me went up to Bangor Street on Friday, and I thought he was a 'silly bugger' as well, when I saw what he was doing. He did not see me, as he placed two red bricks on either side of the front wheel of his bike, taking a long time to measure them up carefully. Leaving another lad in charge of them, so they wouldn't be moved, he rode his bike to the end of the long road. He turned, waited until everyone was watching him; then he started off. Faster and faster he came along Bangor Street, and with all the luck in the world, he rode straight between the two bricks. The crowd of boys, and a few girls, clapped and cheered. He didn't see me there. He did not stop, but just rode away. I did not see him till Sunday. When I spoke to him about it, he said, 'It was nothing!' He was such a slick young guy. I supposed that's what I liked about him.

Miss Holgate said 'Jane Eyre' had been chosen for the school play, to be performed at the end of term, before the Easter holiday. I knew I was going to be Jane. Not one of the girls in the form knew that book like I did. We were going to do the first part of her life, the part where she leaves her Aunt's house, and lives in the orphanage, meeting her friend Helen, who dies with consumption. I rehearsed the part to myself over and over again. On the day the cast was chosen, I could not believe what I was hearing, when a delicate looking girl, with stringy blonde plaits, was chosen to play my beloved Jane, and I was given the part of Helen. I was livid! She couldn't act the part for toffee. I hoped she'd be ill; then I could step in at the very last minute – but she wasn't. On the day of the performance, I gained sympathy from the audience for my part as little Helen, as she slowly faded away. My small part in the play left me squirming as the other girl read the lines I thought should have been mine.

The fun fair came to the town during the Easter holiday. I walked round on the Saturday, after I'd been to the Halifax. Everything was colourful. The lights twinkling, the stall holders shouting at you to try your luck at winning a prize, over the loud noise of music coming from each roundabout. I did not try my hand at trying to win a coconut, or catching toy ducks in a net. I did not waste my spending money on going for a ride on the dragons. Instead, I went to see the manager. I asked him how old you had to be, to join up with the fair people, and travel with them. He looked surprised as he looked me up and down. 'Well, you don't look like you could put up the big wheel, but you seem to be a capable little lass. Why don't you ask again when you are sixteen?'

'Is that the age you have got to be?' I asked.

'I'm afraid so Miss.' I walked away, thinking I might ask him again one day.

New term! Nitty Nora was in school!

Small, bespectacled, with wisps of pale ginger hair peeping from under her nurse's cap, she visited twice a year. Starting at form 1B, she waded her way through all the heads of hair, until she got to 4A, searching for head lice, sending those with, to the school clinic for treatment, and a note to their parents.

I knew I had nits! All the combing with the steel comb we had at home, and all the vinegar was not going to shift them before Nitty Nora got to me. The only thing was to find a

177

reason to be away from school when she inspected 4A.

On the afternoon she was inspecting 3A, I told some of the girls I did not feel so well, to prepare them for my absence next day.

My mother and dad went to work, and my sisters to school. I stayed in the house. I don't know why I didn't try it more often. Nobody at home would have known if I'd been to school or not. At eleven-o-clock there was a knock on the front door. I could hear the familiar voices of the girls from school. I did not answer. They knew I was in! 'Joyce! You've got to come to school. Miss Ellis said.'

I kept quiet. They talked among themselves; then tried again. 'You are not ill. You are only pretending. Come out – or we're telling!'

I still kept quiet. Eventually they went away.

How did they know I wasn't ill? Bloody cheek! I'd show them if I was ill or not – they'd be sorry – and Miss Ellis!

I looked in my medical book, that I'd got from the jumble sale, wondering what illness I could have that would keep me away from school, at least, until Nitty Nora had gone. I decided I would have appendicitis! I would have my appendix out! Spend a lovely time in hospital, in a nice clean bed, and everyone would send me chocolates and flowers.

I looked up the symptoms, and acted them out perfectly. After twenty four hours, even my mother was taken in. Luckily, Dr Mallick was not my doctor. He would have seen right through my little scam. Having lived at my grandma's, in another area, meant I was registered with a doctor at Bastwell. He was sent for – then an ambulance was sent for! I had not eaten anything, except for a half a jar of jam, in the last two days.

When the surgeon, Mr. Pearce came to see me, in my nice

clean bed in the ward, I recited all the symptoms to him. Even when he put on a rubber glove and poked his finger in my bottom, I knew when to say it hurt, and when not.

I was taken to the operating theatre. My appendix was removed.

I was visited later by Mr. Pearce, who said he hadn't found anything wrong with my appendix, but best to be on the safe side. I agreed with him.

I got cards from school, flowers from the Gospel hall, and a postal order from my grandma. Even my parents came to see me after the operation.

'You look a bit glassy eyed, our kid,' my dad said.

I quickly recovered, and helped the nurses. I gave out tea from the tea trolley, and arranged flowers on the lockers. I sang a hymn for the patients on Sunday, bringing tears to their eyes.

The down side of it all was – my boyfriend hadn't sent me a card or been to see me – and – I still had nits! Twice as many as before!

# CHAPTER EIGHTEEN

When Miss Ellis announced that the school leaving year would now be at 15yrs instead of 14yrs, it made me feel down in the dumps for weeks, and my mother wasn't pleased either.

During the long summer holidays, I kept the house clean as usual, but now, my sisters found their own interests, leaving me more time to go to the library, and on other days, out into the country. Dad put my spending money up a few pence, and gave me extra for doing his errands, and making him cups of tea. He allowed me to go to the first house cinema on Saturdays, with my imaginary friends I'd made up, that was really my boyfriend. Seeing as no friends of mine called at our door, it was easy to name friends who didn't exist. I had to be back home at nine. It was their pub night, and my sisters would be left on their own. I had to leave my boyfriend so early on those light summer nights. He was very patient about this, as he left me on the boulevard to get my bus home.

Miss Holgate sensed 4A were not happy to be at school for another year. To cheer us up, she told us school would now be more like being at college. We would have debates, learn another language, and would be given lessons on dress, and make up. In domestic science, more adventurous cookery would be taught, and how to manage household accounts. We would be sent to a large house in St. Alban's Place, owned by the catholic priests, to learn the art of cleaning and running a household.

The debates I enjoyed. The German lessons I struggled

through. 'Pretend you are gargling, girls,' Miss Holgate said. 'It's a gutteral sound'

I was just about able to say 'The Lord's Prayer' in German, by the end of term, which I was pleased about. I thought it would stand me in good stead if they ever started fighting us again. I imagined them barging into our house, their bayonets fixed, and I would calm them down by saying the prayer of prayers to them – in German!

Miss Ellis gave lessons in dress and make up. She wore a fine powder on her face, and the lightest touch of lipstick, not Tangee or Ponds.

She told us never to wear more than three colours at a time. We must pay special attention to gloves and shoes. A hat must always be worn in church, and of course, smoking was a filthy habit.

At last, in my final year at school, I could choose not to play hockey, and escaped from that long walk to the cold playing fields.

The domestic science room, where we cooked baked apples and custard, rock cakes and jam tarts, was warm and welcoming on cold days. Miss Smith, the teacher, plump and comfortable in her white apron and cap that kept her straight dark hair hidden, taught us how to cook, and make exceptional good coffee for the teachers and for the girls in her class. My cookery was limited, because I could never take the full amount of money for the ingredients. I was mostly chosen to make the coffee. I became good at coffee making, with full cream milk provided, and made sure I drank my share of it in the process.

The cookery exam had been arranged, the marks we got

would be recorded in our last report, that we had to show to our respective employers when we left school to start work.

Miss Smith had given us a list of ingredients we would need to bring to the class, along with our washed and ironed green pinafores and caps.

I tried for days to get the ingredients for my meat pie and sponge cake I was to make. Letty had taken a few things from her mother's larder for me, but I still hadn't enough.

On the morning of the exam, I anticipated Miss Smith inspecting the few things I had brought; then sending me to Miss Ellis.

I had to think of an alternative.

If needs must, the devil drives, my grandma would have said. After seeing my sisters off to school, I sat at the kitchen table and decided. I could not take the cookery exam!

Feeling weak at the knees, I picked up the bread knife, and sliced my hand with it, just under my left thumb. Luckily we had some old bandages that my dad had brought home with him when he left the army. I carefully bandaged my left hand, letting the blood soak through; then went to school to face Miss Smith.

Without much sympathy, I was sent into form 3B, to read a book, while the other girls cooked. The delicious smell of pies, cakes and coffee, wafted along the school corridors.

There was a blank space for 'domestic science' on my end of school report.

Twice my mother had disappeared for a couple of days. We didn't ask questions when dad said she had got a bit annoyed with him and gone to stay with a friend. He'd come home early from work on those days, lit the fire, and made our tea, before going out for a while. When he returned, he would sit with us, and tell us how life was going to be better for us all. There would be no more arguments. We would have days out into the country together. We would have family holidays to lovely places. He described the pretty villages and seaside resorts he'd been to during the war, promising to take us there. I believed him. It was nice just to have him on his own, without my mother. He didn't go to the pub. The domestic scene felt safe and secure.

It was some time after our mother's return, that we found out, each time she'd gone away, she had been taken in an ambulance after putting her head in the gas oven, after we had left for school. No wonder the neighbours felt sorry for us. One time she went away to a convalescent home in Blackpool for three weeks. When she came back, she brought photos of herself, and the people and staff she had met there. On the photos, she had her arm in a sling. We didn't ask why.

Gilbert and Sullivan were not on my list of favourite composers. Their quick and witty words did nothing for me. I preferred the romance of Tchaikowsky or the strength of Wagner that Miss Holgate introduced me to. Yet when I heard they wanted singers at the local Youth Club, to perform in a Gilbert and Sullivan production, I was keen to go. It wasn't Letty's scene. So my first ever visit to a youth club, was with a group of girls from school, also interested in drama. I was not attracted to the crowd of the club. The hustle and bustle of loud laughter and conversation, I looked on from a distance.

For weeks I went along, to take my part with two other girls while we rehearsed the 'Three Little Maids from School.' The costumes, vibrant in colour, were wonderful. We three little maids practiced using our beautiful lace fans, while we sang our words in perfect unison. The producer took it all very seriously. He wanted the show to be the talk of the town. We must attend all rehearsals, learn the words of the script without stumbling over them, and keep quiet when he was talking.

I managed to leave the club early, to be home at the time dad had stipulated. Just a few days to go before the show went on stage, costumes chosen, stage lighting fixed, programmes printed.

On the Sunday of the final rehearsal, I missed meeting my boyfriend, as we rehearsed all afternoon. I told my dad I was rehearsing. He told me to be back home at nine o clock. As I sang my Three Little maids…I watched the fingers on the clock on the club wall go slowly round. It was coming up for nine, and we had to go through the last scenes again. 'Nobody leaves now!' the director told me, when I asked to go. I was not too worried. Dad would be in the pub with my mother. I would be home and in bed before they got back. Just after ten o clock, the director let us go, with a list of final instructions for the first night of the show.

I hadn't ironed my dad's white overalls, but I didn't care. He would have to wear them creased, and I would have to wear a creased school blouse next day. I ran all the way home, along the range and down Freme Street. I knew my sisters would be in bed, in the house alone.

When I got to the front door, I noticed the light was on in the parlour. I went in, out of breath from running.

My dad was sitting in an armchair. He was dressed in his best suit. My mother was out. He stared at me in silence for a moment; then in a quiet voice asked, 'And where do you think you have been?'

I told him – to the youth club, rehearsing. I told him, we

had rehearsed all day. He knew where I had been. He stood up slowly, and took off his broad leather belt from around his waist. He swung it up into the air, bringing it down striking the wooden table that stood under the window with it. He came to me and hit the side of my face with his open hand. He didn't strike me with the belt. He kept hitting the table with it. I moved out of his way, as he followed me about the room. The crack of the leather on the wooden table made me jump each time he brought it down. His mouth was white, his bottom lip thrust forward. He came to me and put his face close to mine. 'If you ever dare to disobey me again, I will whip you within one inch of your life – and – you can forget all about the youth club from now.'

I knew I was wetting my knickers in fear. I scrambled upstairs out of his way. He hadn't been out to the pub that night. He'd just sat waiting for me.

I undressed in the dark, shivering and whimpering, glad to hide under the darkness of the grey blanket and old khaki army coat.

I did not enter the youth club again. Letty went to tell the director I could not be in the show. I'd let him and the rest of the cast down very badly. Someone else had to stand in for me at the very last minute.


We got off the tram at Wilpshire, and walked hand in hand through the field of buttercups and daisies. My boyfriend said he had something to tell me. When a boy said that to a girl on the films, he meant he was going to ask her to marry him, or he was going to finish with her.

We sat down on the sweet soft grass. I started to make a daisy chain. 'I've got my call up papers for my national service.

I'm going in the R.A.F in a few months time,' was what he had waited till then to tell me. I could not believe he was leaving me. He insisted he wouldn't be, that nothing would change. I tried to believe him, but my fairy godmother was tapping me on my shoulder. 'Don't believe him, my dear,' she whispered. 'I'm afraid he's going to be the first of the philanderers you will know!' I brushed my fairy godmother aside, as he kissed me among the buttercups, and I kissed him back with all my girlish heart.

Twelve of us were leaving school at Easter. A careers mistress from the education office came to school to talk to us.

She sat at Miss Holgate's desk, with a list of our names in her hand. 'I will work through the list, and suggest a job you may be suited to, with the information I have collected from the school, and your reports. After, I shall stay and answer any questions you may have,' she told us.

She started in alphabetical order. Reading out their names, she started with the first two girls on the list, suggesting typing in a solicitor's office in Richmond Terrace. The next girl, she suggested shop work for, the Co-operative Society were looking for bright girls. She then got to my name on her list. She read it out, and I put up my hand to let her know it was me. 'Yes, I've got you down here. You will be going to work in Swallow Street Mill. That is the nearest mill to your home, isn't it?' I felt myself go hot. I stood up. 'I'm not going into the mill,' I told her firmly. I am going to be a nurse!' I sat down again. She hesitated for the briefest of seconds; then said, 'Perhaps you can see me at the end.' She went on to the next name on her list.

The girls crowded round the desk with excitement, to ask

questions about how and when they should apply for their new jobs, how much the wages were etc;

I walked out of the classroom and into the schoolyard. I did not wait to speak to her. No way was I going into the bloody mill! She could keep her lousy job. I would find a job myself!

Letty and me linked our arms as we walked round and round the edge of the huge playing field up on' tops. The nights were drawing in. Little did we know that would be our last walk in that field together. We sat down for a while in the dusk of the cool evening. The ground was cold and hard, as we exchanged our confidences, and laughed, as we talked about people, things – and boys!

When I got home, I realized with a sinking feeling, I had lost my front door key. The small Yale key must have fallen out of my gymslip pocket as we sat on the grass

Before dad left for work next morning, I was up and dressed. I had to have a key to get in the house after school, to let my sisters in, and light the fire. I asked him if I could borrow his key. He told me I could not. I had to tell him I had lost mine. I was told to find it, or – not to come home at all!

That day was cold and windy. A day to wear cardigans, scarves, wool socks, and gloves if you had them. I didn't stay for my school dinner. While the other girls filed into the dining room, I left and walked up to the playing field. In the biting cold, I walked round, trying to retrace the steps where I had walked the night before with Letty. There were no other people about. Dinner break was nearly over. School was a long way off. It was nearly time to make my way back there. I looked one more time at the space, slightly flattened, where I'd sat with Letty. If I don't find it, where should I go, I asked myself. He told me not to go back home. It was then I saw it – There was my key! Lying in the grass and mud. I thanked God, with a sigh of relief. I ran back along London Road and down Calder Street in time to hear the bell ringing in the school playground.

I had stopped going to Sunday School. My boyfriend had reluctantly continued to go for some time, mainly to appease his religious mother. I still saw him on Sundays.

It was after one of our long walks, when arriving back home, that my mother said to me, 'You are in trouble! Your dad is going to kill you! That lad you have been bothering with has written things in his diary about you. His mother has been down and shown it to your dad. She made him read it! I'm warning you. He'll kill you when he gets in!'

'I haven't done anything!' I protested.

'O' No? Well, we'll see about that. You are going to find yourself in a ditch with a stocking round your neck. That's where you are going to end up. Another thing – you have not to see that lad again!'

Dad was out working, even though it was Sunday. Somebody had asked him to paint a ceiling!

I waited in fear. I heard the familiar sound of his motorbike come through the backyard gate. It stopped. He came through the shed at the back of the house, and into the back living room. He dropped his kit bag that he carried his snap box and overalls in, onto the floor, and glanced across at me. I was too afraid to speak. His bottom lip dropped down into a sneer, as he passed me to go to the sink for his wash. He did not speak to me. He did not say one word. He did not say one word to me for another three months! He totally ignored me. It was accepted by my mother and sisters that this was how it was to be. When they talked together, he excluded me. It would have been better if he had given me a hiding. When he did speak to me again, he never ever mentioned the incident of the diary. Neither did I.

Defiantly I still met my boyfriend! We met in secret places. We went on the tramcar separately. I would sit downstairs, he on top deck. We sat together in the darkness of the cinema on Saturday night. He had suffered at home, but not in the way I had. He'd written in his diary that we had kissed in the field of buttercups – his mother had wrung her hands and prayed for his sins!

At last my parents had made friends! They'd met at the pub. A couple about their own age, who only lived two streets away. They called at our house before they all went out together. It was lovely to see someone in our house. We didn't visit or have people for tea, like other ordinary families did. My mother had not seen her family very often since dad's return from the army. He did not like her family. I loved seeing dad jovial and friendly, and my mother smiling and laughing with them. It was good for her to have another woman to talk to.

It didn't last! After a few weeks and after hearing my dad call them all the names under the sun to my mother, they stopped seeing them. Once more our home was closed to the outside world.

# CHAPTER NINETEEN

What I thought was going to be the most wonderful day of my life, came and went without ceremony. My last day at school!

Miss Ellis gave us a talk about what she thought were worldly things. Miss Holgate gave us our school reports to take to our new employers.

I had really tried with my homework during the last term. Apart from math's I'd really made a big effort to get good marks. Out of the twelve of us who were leaving school, I was bitterly disappointed to come eighth in position. Miss Ellis had written on my report that I had tried, but it had been impossible for me to reach a higher standard, due to having had six weeks off school during the last year, through illness!

We cleared our desks, and handed in our books. It was time to walk out of the classroom and into the big world. The girls were abuzz, talking about their new jobs, kissing each other goodbye, and crying. They were going in a group to say fond farewells to Miss Ellis and the other teachers. They had little cards and presents to give to thank them for their kindness over the last few years.

I collected the small dictionary my grandad had given to me, and the small green tea apron I'd managed to make in the sewing class. Putting them in my tatty brown satchel, that I would need no more – I left! I walked along the corridor for the last time, to the outside door. I didn't look back, as I thought about the misery I'd sometimes endured there. Gone now were those cold days when I shivered in my damp thin blouse, and shoes with cardboard in the soles. Gone were the days when other girls lent to me a cardigan, a school tie, a cap, a pair of pumps. Gone were the days when I dreaded having to do PE because my navy blue school knickers were hanging off me, and when my period had started, I'd pieces of rag or newspaper in them, as my mother thought one sanitary towel could last me five days. Goodbye Bangor Street Girl's School! I would not appreciate you, or the guidance of the good teachers there for many years.

I felt a freedom I had never experienced before, as I left the school grounds, alone. I half ran, half skipped down Freme Street, getting home early, to light the fire.

I was due to start work in the winding shed at Swallow Street Mill on Monday morning.

'You're going, Lady!' my mother said. 'Is it not good enough for you or something? It had to be good enough for me. It's £3 a week. That's good money. Jimmy Melody has had your name down for over a year now. You are lucky he's taking you on.'

I didn't care if Jimmy Melody, the overseer at the mill had my name down since the day I was born. I wasn't going in the mill! She knew I wanted to be a nurse, well, an actress really, but that seemed a long way off now, so a nurse would have to do. Dad did not persuade me to go into the mill. He just said, 'Listen! There are thousands of cells in the body, and you haven't the brains to learn one of them!'

They went out to the pub. I went to tell Letty all about it. We decided, if I got up early on Saturday morning, I could go into the town and look for a job. If I got one, I wouldn't have to go into the mill.

I was ready very early, making myself look as employable

as I could. Neat and tidy like Miss Ellis had told us, but I'm afraid – no gloves.

Letty could not come with me. She was staying on at school for another year. Her homework was abounding, and her parents saw to it that she did it.

First, I took myself into Boot's Chemist, on Church Street, as soon as the doors opened at nine am. The manager directed me into his office, and asked me the usual questions. I was doing well, speaking in the voice my grandma had taught me, until he asked me to add up some figures in my head. I had to pretend he was a customer. Checkouts, calculators and tills that showed how much change to give, had not come into being then. My mind went blank. I imagined Miss Heaps glaring at me. I got them wrong. He asked me, if I could choose, what counter in the shop would I prefer to work on. I told him, the surgical counter. I thought for a moment I'd got the job by saying that. He said he needed someone for the photography counter!

I hadn't got the job!

Next on my list, was the Telephone Exchange at the General Post Office on Darwen Street. The supervisor, a thin spindly, kindly woman, with rimless spectacles on a chain hanging down on her black dress, led me down a corridor, and into a room she described as 'the heart of it all.'

She told me to wait. As I did, I watched the girl telephonists, their ears covered with small speakers attached to wires in a box in front of them. The confusion of conversation was worse than the noise in the weaving and winding sheds at the mill.

I looked up at the tiny window, letting in an unfair share of light. I could not see myself there for eight hours a day. I left!

The morning was flying by. I had exactly one hour before my destiny was sealed forever – to spend my life in Swallow Street Mill.

I was really scraping the barrel when I walked up the stone steps of the Sewing Machine Factory in Randall Street. I could not even use a sewing machine properly. I was good at darning, but that wasn't going to count.

Once again I saw a supervisor, and once more I was told to wait. I waited in the stone flagged corridor, next to a large green door, with small square windows. Tipping up on my toes, I managed to see through the windows. My heart sank as I saw about fifty huge black iron sewing machines, in rows, like army tanks.

I fled down the stone steps and back into the street.

My last call in the few minutes I had left of the morning, was to the Health Office, next to the school clinic, on Victoria Street. The receptionist on duty, said Miss Brown, the Nursing Supervisor for clinics and day nurseries, did not give interviews on Saturday mornings, and advised me to write in for an interview. I had not thought of becoming a nursery nurse. My ambition was to work in hospital, but anything was better than the mill.

It was pleading time! I laid all my cards on the table, giving one of the best and truest performances of my life. I made her see me, pale and thin, chained to a weaving machine, in my black brat and clogs. She was truly moved, and took me to Miss Brown's office. Miss Brown agreed to see me. A small serious woman dressed in a white uniform coat, over a navy blue skirt and pale blue blouse, with her S.R.N badge pinned to its collar. Her navy hat covered her tight dark curls. She was a no nonsense type! She heard me out, asking few questions.

I could start at St. Alban's Day Nursery on Monday morning at seven am! I could have kissed her! The wage would be twenty five shillings a week from Monday to Saturday. I would have a medical later. I would be called 'Nurse!'

My dad said nothing. My mother went mad! Twenty five measly shillings, when I could have earned three pounds a week.

At seven in the morning on a cold spring day, I presented myself at the large house in St. Alban's Place. A house that had belonged to St. Alban's Roman Catholic Church to house their priests, but had now been turned into a day nursery for the children of the working mothers in the area.

I was given a royal blue overall to wear. I was shown how to fold and secure my nurses cap. To pin it at the nape of my neck, so that it fell into a triangle, just like the one my nurse had worn on the knitting pattern in the wool shop at Bastwell many years ago.

My first job was to light the fire in the massive black leaded iron grate in the downstairs room known as 'the tweenies room.' I placed round it the biggest fireguard I had ever seen, before laying the small dining tables with tiny cereal bowls and small spoons, in readiness for the hot porridge that was brought from the kitchen, to be given to the 'tweenies,' the two year olds, who would come to us, cold, and still tired, having been lifted from their cots so early in the day, for their mothers to earn the money to keep them by working in the surrounding mills.

If I started work at seven in the morning, I left at four in the afternoon. If I started at nine, I left at six in the evening.

My last duty of the day when on that shift, was to mop the floors of the large playrooms and toilets. Even though the work was hard, I was happier on the late shift. It meant I got out of lighting the fire, and preparing the tea at home.

On Saturdays dad had to go to the Halifax himself now, as the morning was taken up for me, cleaning the nursery from top to bottom. We even scrubbed the scrubbing brushes. My hands were red and sore. The nurses took it in turn to wash and iron the nurse's caps for the following week. They had to be crisply starched. We all feared the starch we made would not set properly. Matron's cap was small and frilly. I had nightmares of it being floppy when she put it on her head on the following Monday, or scorching it while I was ironing it as carefully as I could.

When I handed my mother my very first wage packet containing twenty five shillings, she was not amused. Like my dad, I didn't get a thank you. She decided to give me 2/6d back out of it.

Matron told me I needed black shoes and stockings for my uniform, white ankle socks would not be permitted. I bought my first pair of black woolly stockings from Tunstall's drapery shop, and a chocolate bar from Mrs. Ward's toffee shop with my first wage. Luckily, I had black shoes, from the jumble sale.

I wrote to my grandma, telling her I'd started work, and all about my duties at the nursery. She sent me a supply of black stockings that lasted me for months.

Coming home from the nursery one afternoon at four-o-clock, I passed the terraced houses at the end of Enamel Street. There was nobody about. Something in one of the bedroom windows of the small end house caught my eye. I looked up – and there I saw him. The husband of my parent's ex friends, the one who'd been to our house, who had been friendly with my dad. The husband of the nice woman my mother got on with, the one who worked as a cleaner at the cinema. He had his pants down, and was exposing himself for all he was worth. I looked – aghast! If only Letty had been with me. We would have given him a right mouthful. 'What do you call that?' Letty would have shouted. I was too shocked to do anything but look away and walk quickly on. He obviously had not got to know my dad very well during the short time they'd been so called friends. My dad would rip him apart, limb from limb when I told him.

But – I didn't tell my dad, or my mother. I thought better of it. I only told Letty!


Risks, I learned, had become worth taking – well, some!

I risked being 'whipped within one inch of my life,' if my dad found out I let my boyfriend in the house when he and my mother went to the Star Cinema, and my sisters were in bed on Tuesday and Thursday nights. That risk wasn't worth taking really, as we sat on the settee in the freezing cold parlour, listening for footsteps coming down the street, always thinking we could hear my parents coming back. We would jump up, and run through the living room, into the backyard, and out of the back gate. I would laugh my socks off, when we realized it was not them at all. I loved the thrill of it!

After a few weeks, my boyfriend decided we would meet outside of the house in future. So on those nights, I left my sisters alone, getting back home just before my parents.

I took the risk of making up imaginary friends I'd made at the nursery, so that I had an excuse to go to imaginary places with them. I described to my dad, in detail, exactly where I was going, what times, and with whom, while I met my boyfriend, and we went to the cinema.

I invented lectures to attend, demonstrations of child care, visits to clinics, sometimes true, sometimes not, in order to stay out of the house more and more

The work at the day nursery was enjoyable, but tiring. The three storey converted house made the physical side of it, very hard. The youngest babies were in the nursery on the top floor, the tweenies on the first floor, and the toddlers on the ground floor. The kitchen and laundry were in the basement. If the children went to play in the large yard area, that adjoined the cellars, everything they needed had to be transported down there. Potties, extra pants and nappies, flannels, towels, drinks, mugs, biscuits, sand pit and water play. At the end of the day, it was all carted back inside of the house again, the toys then washed in disinfectant, the dirty pants sluiced and laundered, the yard itself swept and swilled.

Miss Brown arranged my compulsory medical as she'd promised. I attended the Health Office, and was seen by the medical officer. There was some concern about the attacks of jaundice I'd suffered from in the past. I was advised on the benefits of eating a healthier diet. This was impossible at home. I'd eaten a diet saturated in fat since being small. Most of our meals were fried in thick white lumps of lard. Eggs, bread, sausage, pies from Jennings, and bags of battered bits from the chip shop, started to clog up my young arteries without me knowing.

Miss Brown gave us lectures that led to the qualification of a Nursery Nurse. My very first lecture was held in my old school on Whalley Range, now known as The People's College.

I sat in the same classroom where I had made my Christmas card for my grandma, and where the boy had borrowed my red crayon, and never given it back.

The first notes of my very first lecture, written in my very first lecture book, were…

'Food is taken into the mouth, torn and chewed by the teeth, mixed with the saliva which softens it; is rolled into a ball by the tongue, taken to the back of the mouth, and swallowed.'

I felt like a real student. A college student! It was to be the first lecture of a hundred or so that I would take down in the next few years. Some I would retain in my mind easily. Some I would have a struggle to understand, and some I would hardly hear at all, as I would go straight to them, after a twelve hour shift on night duty on the busy hospital wards, to sit at a desk, listening to the tutor drawning on in the background, while I tried to keep my eyes open.

Dad had decorated our house all the way through. New net curtains had been hung at all the windows. The back yard had been tidied up, and a proper toilet roll placed behind the door of the toilet outside. On arriving home a few days later, I found a middle aged couple in the house, shaking hands with my mother and dad. They'd been sent from the council offices to view our rented house in Freme Street, with the intention of exchanging tenancies. Their council property was up Little Harwood, on the new estate. I heard them say they missed the friendliness of the people in the back streets, and the garden adjoining their house was to much work for them to manage.

Large airy rooms, big windows, separate kitchen,

bathroom with toilet! And – three bedrooms! A room for me!

My parents had already seen the house. It was all signed and sealed within a matter of days. We were moving!

Dad borrowed a van, and took a day off work. While I was at the day nursery, they moved. I went home to a new address.

Over the previous few days, I only had time to see Letty once. We hugged, and promised we would see each other soon. We would still meet. We would go to the market, to the library. I would watch her swim in the school galas. We would go up the fields on summer evenings. We would always be friends.

I left Freme Street – and – I never saw Letty again!

From streets to avenues and crescents, skirted with young green trees and grass verges. At the tip of the town, elevated, out of the smoke. Bleak in winter but reached by the sun in summer. Children played in the large gardens, while parents grew their own vegetables, and had barbecues for their friends on warm evenings, - apart from my parents!

We enjoyed our new house. My sisters shared the back bedroom, with a view over the town and dark hills beyond. I enjoyed the privacy of my small room, and a cupboard on the landing, where I hung my clothes. I still covered my bed with my dad's old khaki army coat. It was somehow, warm and comforting. Dad broke up the old jerry pots and threw them in the dustbin. The bathroom was a luxury. We even had a second toilet outside, and a shed for dad's motorbike. He was happy in his role of homemaker. He decorated parts of the house, while singing or whistling the song he always sang or whistled, while painting – 'With a Million Little Stars I Could Decorate the Ceiling'

When he was happy, my mother was happy – so we were happy – well, for a few weeks at least.

The crescent was a long way from the shops, but that did not worry me now, as my sisters did the shopping. It was also further from St. Alban's Day Nursery. To be there at seven in the morning, meant I had to get up very early. My clip curls that I now put up in my hair every night took ages to take down in the morning, but they curled my hair beautifully, and I promised myself I would never have straight hair again.

Miss Brown was very understanding when I gave her my new address. She transferred me to Churchill House Day Nursery. This was a large house, in its own grounds, not far from my home. Situated across from the memorial gardens. It had been the home and surgery of the doctor my grandad had been seen by, on the night during the blackout, when he had fallen into the gardens, and broken his nose.

I had become an expert at domestic pursuits. Not only at the nursery, but at home. We still had lists of jobs to be done, made out by dad. I think he thought I was a horse! Not being a gardener of any sorts, he allocated the gardening to me. He had big ideas of a huge orderly vegetable garden on one side of the house, smooth lawns at front and back, edged with magnificent flowers and shrubs. I nearly broke my back one day, as he'd left orders for me to dig over the large plot of land. It took me all day. When he got home from work that night, he told me I'd made a mess of it! I vowed to myself never to touch the garden again. He could dig his own bloody garden in future.

## CHAPTER TWENTY

The bus stop was at the end of the long road, and took twenty minutes to get into the town, where on Saturdays, I now met my boyfriend, under the statue of Queen Victoria, on Blackburn Boulevard. I was allowed out until 10 pm, meaning I had to get the bus half an hour earlier to be home on time. I still had my imaginary friends to fall back on, if asked by my parents, where I was going, but I was seldom asked.

To my delight, I discovered there was a concert party in the town, belonging to the Queen's Hall Methodist Church . A young nurse at the nursery told me all about it, and we decided we would join. Of course, it would mean attending the church service on a Sunday, but anything to get into a concert party! We started to go to the services, and being talented we were both soon invited to join the concert group. We took to the stage, singing our hearts out, mimicking the old tyme music hall stars, and doing the 'Can Can' together in our black stockings and frilly skirts and knickers.

I'd roped my boyfriend into joining the church. He tolerated the religious side, and although he wasn't in the concert party, came to watch, without comment.

One Sunday evening, after the service, the three of us stood together outside of the hall. I was upset, because the night before, he had stood me up. I'd waited and waited for him in the freezing cold weather, under the statue of Queen Victoria, before I got the bus back home. If only we'd had mobile phones, maybe life would have been much easier.

He did not give me much of an explanation as to why he had not kept our date. I suppose it was a bit embarrassing for him, in front of another girl. He was as cocky and as cool as always. He asked me, 'Are you coming for a walk or not?' I was still upset. 'I don't know!' I said.

He then turned to the other girl, and asked her – 'Would you like to come for a walk with me?' 'Yes!,' she told him, - and off they walked together, leaving me standing there!

'What did I tell you?' whispered my fairy godmother.

It was the beginning of the end of my first romance.

During the next few months fate would decide that we would part. He would join the R.A.F. I would enter hospital as a junior nurse. His mother would even invite me to tea – but then we would go our separate ways.

Miss Brown was very cross when I told her I wanted to leave the day nursery, and become a cadet nurse at Queen's Park Hospital.

'Why are you girls always in such a hurry? Eighteen months to gain your N.N.E.B is not long at all; then you can go into hospital to do your general nursing training. You will then have an extra qualification at your fingertips.' I knew Miss Brown was right, but she did not live at our house, and eighteen months seemed a lifetime to me. I knew I could perhaps, one day, live in the nurse's home, if I worked in hospital. It was my plan to do that, and leave home as soon as I was able.

I received a letter from matron at Queen's Park Hospital, in reply to the one I had sent to her, asking if I could become a cadet nurse. She sent me a date for an interview.

I had also been to the police station, to ask what age I had to be before I could leave home. The police officer had led me into his office, behind a row of dark prison cells. I'd only seen prison cells with bars on the films. I walked behind the officer, glancing in each one. I did not see any prisoners, but I did think to myself – If my dad could see me now!

'Sixteen! – Officially!' the police officer told me. 'That's the age when you can leave home. But, if you do anything silly, your parents can take you back. If I were you, I would wait until you are seventeen.' He did not ask me any questions. I thanked him, and left, walking quickly through the main doors, hoping nobody I knew would see me coming out.

My dad was proud of me, I think, but didn't show it. Yet, he gave me fifteen pounds to buy a smart navy blue Gaberdine coat, and to pay for my nursing text books, when I had passed my interview and had been accepted as a student nurse. I read my letter from matron over and over. There was a list of rules I was sure I would adhere to. Nurses were never to be seen in the street without their outdoor cap. Black shoes and stockings must be worn at all times. The list of rules was endless, but the most interesting thing was the date and time I had to present myself for duty.

My grandma sent me a huge supply of black stockings, and although thick wool, I did not care. I was grateful.

My first steps into the long female surgical ward, known as E1 ward, were the first steps into my new life. In my stiffly starched uniform of purple and white stripes, complete with apron and butterfly cap, I timidly performed my very first nursing task, giving out the small green salt and pepper pots to each patient, placing them carefully on their bedside table – and so my nursing career had begun.

I was given one day a week off duty. The ward sister chose that day to be Mondays, the same day off that she took herself. 'It's because she likes you,' said some of the seniors. 'It's because she wants to keep an eye on you,' said the others.

I worked hard, leaving home early and returning late. My life was now the hospital. I stayed on duty all day if we were short of staff. I don't know where I got the energy from. On Saturdays I would work twelve hours; then walk down the long hill with the other staff going off duty, to get my bus at the boulevard, home to Little Harwood.

My wages of twelve pounds a month, were given to my mother, in the small brown envelope I received them in. She gave me £2 back. I argued with her that my bus fare was 4/3d a week, leaving me nothing for anything else, but it fell on deaf ears. On my one day off a week, I cleaned the house. My mother had left the mill, but still worked full time at a local factory making parts for radio and televisions. The rows between my parents had started again on Saturday nights. Moving into a better home made no difference to who had smoked the most Woodbines, or who had kissed who in the pub.

Our new neighbours were beginning to feel sorry for us three girls. The walls between the semi detached houses were thin. I felt ashamed when I met the couple next door, who had two lovely children, and who must have been able to hear the dreadful carryings on.

Yet another medical had to be got through, this time by the staff medical officer at the hospital.

A group of new nurses stood together, in pants and bra, waiting to be weighed, x rayed and given various kinds of inoculations. A tall busty blonde nurse made fun of my neat small breasts. I would often think of her in later years, as I put on my same size petite bras, wondering how she made out with her pendulous contraptions.

Again, concern was raised about my bouts of jaundice, and my weight of only 6st. 10lbs. I was put on a low fat diet that was easy to follow, as my main meals were now prepared in the hospital kitchen, and served to me in the nurse's dining room, during my long spells on duty. The special diet did not go down well with my ward sister, when she saw me eating chicken, while she was served minced meat. Her voice drifted over to my table, as I heard her saying – 'Who does that one think she is? Chicken indeed!'

My liver decided it was time to put me through another yellowing experience, low fat diet or not. This meant two weeks off duty, which I hated. I was only happy tramping the wards. Yet I wasn't well, and found it hard to eat anything at all, as well as feeling depressed about looking like a chink. Having to stay in the house gave me the opportunity to follow a pursued plan I'd embarked on. I'd decided when I left school that my education was not as complete as I would have liked. During the months that followed I had picked up books, promising myself that I would read what I thought I had missed out on. I'd collected most of the classics and the full works of Shakespeare. In my small box room, I hid myself away, reading into the small hours, catching up on things I realized I should have paid more attention to at school, or if I'd have been lucky, to have had more help with at home. I made a promise to myself, even when I returned to the hospital, I would continue these studies. I did this for the next year, and was very proud of my achievement and self discipline.

We still had to put up with dad's wrath about one thing or another when he got home from the pub on Saturday afternoons. He taunted us. This time, it was my turn -

My bout of jaundice was lasting longer than usual. I had been poorly with it for three weeks, before it showed signs of abating. My dad was unsympathetic. 'There is nothing wrong with you! You haven't got jaundice. It's all in the mind and I'm going to prove it to you,' he told me. He went into the kitchen, and came back into the living room with a huge fatty meat pie in his hand. 'I dare you to eat this,' he said, handing me the pie. To look at it, nearly made me vomit. I knew he'd had a lot to drink. I refused. 'I haven't to have anything fatty,' I told him quietly. 'I dare you,' he said. 'Go on! I dare you!' I refused again. 'You – are lilly livered,' he told me. 'That's the only thing wrong with you.'

I took the meat pie from his hand, and ate it! The whole lot!

A few hours later, I was violently ill.

A whole new world had been opened up before me. I heard and saw things most teenagers would never experience. I learned strict discipline. I listened in now, to the conversations of intelligent persons. I walked behind the consultants as they visited their patients – Mr. Dunlop, the surgeon, handsome Mr. Ward, the medical consultant, Mr. Jack, the orthopaedic surgeon, who I would assist in the operating theatre in time to come. I learned to control my emotions, to be practical and level headed when required. I learned to laugh easily, and to develop the sense of humour and fun, passed on to me from my grandma.

Some duties I would never like. One of them was escorting patients to the operating theatre. I felt the fear that was going on inside of their heads, as the staff made little jokes with them, trying to put them at their ease. As I left them at the theatre doors, I promised them all would be well, it would all be over very soon. I would go back to the ward, and make their bed, I promised I would be waiting for them, and would look after them upon their return. I realized – I would never make a surgical nurse!

While the other nurses were dancing in King George's Hall on Saturday nights, I stayed working on the wards, but I did love the Friday night hops within the hospital, that I tried to attend, telling my dad I had to work very late. Kicking my heels in a strapless black gown, with the boy I was going to marry was still in the distance.

As I left the hospital ward in the evenings, after saying a polite – 'Good night, Sister! Thank you, Sister!' to the ward sister, I watched with envy as the nurses who lived in the nurse's home, wrapped their navy blue and red cloaks around their shoulders, and walked together up to the home. I envied them their companionship, and their freedom.

Another incident at home pushed me further into the plans I had been making for a very long time – to leave.

During a spell of duties on the women's medical ward, I was asked by the ward sister to make up a bed ready to admit a patient. An oxygen cylinder would be needed and a mouth tray. I completed the task, and awaited the arrival of the patient, whoever, who was being brought in by ambulance.

An hour later, the sister told me to make up the bed again; then to see her in her office. Putting the oxygen cylinder back into the corridor where it was stored, and clearing my mouth tray in the small bathroom where we kept the trays, bowls and instruments, I wondered what I had done wrong.

I went to the office and knocked. Sister asked me in, and closed the door behind me. She told me – the patient was being brought to the hospital by ambulance, when she had made a great fuss, and utterly refused to come to Queen's Park Hospital. She had even tried to get off the trolley and out of the ambulance. She'd had to be restrained by the ambulance staff, and had been taken to Blackburn Infirmary instead.

The reason she had given for not wanting to be admitted to Q.P.H. was that her daughter was a nurse there. Sister told me the name of the patient.

My mother had been found in the back garden of our house, after trying to gas herself again. The neighbours had called the ambulance. I had made up a hospital bed for my own mother!

This was an opportunity to tell the sister of the conditions at home, and my intention to move into the nurse's home at the given time. I was sent to matron, to relate to her my situation. Matron said there would be a room in the home for me when I was ready.

After a week, my mother was discharged from the infirmary. On the day she was due home, I spoke to a male nurse I'd confided in, about the difficulty of seeing her again, and what I should say. 'You can only ask her how she feels now,' he advised. 'Are you feeling better?' As a nurse, that should come easy.'

But it didn't come easy. There was a tense atmosphere as I went into the house, and saw her sitting in her usual armchair. She did not speak as I walked over to her. 'Are you feeling better?' I asked. I knew the question was cold and stilted. I should have been able to put my arms about her, and hold her, and say to her – 'Mum, please Mum don't do anything like that again.'

'I'm alright!' she replied. That was that.

She did not tell me she had made a fuss in the ambulance.

She would never know I had made the bed up for her admittance.

Suffering all the pitfalls of being a student, I went through the humiliating experiences that students have to put up with. I was sent to the operating theatre for the fallopian tubes. I was asked to look in a bedpan to see if the patient had passed flatus. It happens to all of us!

I had great fun joining the hospital concert party, as we made fools of ourselves on stage. The hours I spent at rehearsals, in fits of laughter with the other very amateur performers, I told my dad I was working. I even managed to sleep over, staying with my new friend Ursula, in her tiny room, where she was resident. 'I'm on a very late shift,' I would tell my dad. 'It will be impossible for me to get the last bus home.'

This was my first taste of freedom. I was loving it!

Before the Friday night hop, that was held in the main hall, near to the doctor's rooms, we nurses carefully ironed our black dirndl skirts that were in fashion, and our white organdie blouses. We lent and swapped clothes with each other. We ironed for the nurses who were in bed during the day after their night on duty. We all got ready at once, hammering on the cold, shared bathrooms, telling each other to hurry up. We shared a one and only razor between us, shaving under our arms. We borrowed shampoo, lipsticks, shoes and handbags. It was a great feeling. I could not wait for the day when I could live in the nurse's home.

'I'm falling behind in my studies,' I told my dad. 'The hours are too long. I do not get my lectures in on time.' I had droned on like this to him for weeks, setting the stage for when I asked him if I could leave home to live in. One Friday night, it came to the crunch. I always waited to spring things on my parents if I wanted anything, or ask for things in a casual manner, as if it really did not matter. Friday night was pay night and pub night. Usually the mood was good – well, at the start of the night.

They were almost ready to go out. I seized the opportunity. I'd rehearsed it again and again. I tried to make it sound casual –

'Will it be alright if I lived in the nurse's home,' I asked my dad.

'No!' he said at once. 'It won't be alright!' My mother glared at me, saying nothing.

'Well, matron sent for me today,' I lied. ' She said I might have to give up nursing if I don't live in, because my classroom work isn't up to standard. With the travelling to and from home, I don't have the time. It would be better if I lived in. Nearly all the student nurses live in.'

He listened as I rambled on. He ignored me, and went upstairs to continue to get ready for his night out. I was left standing by the fire in the living room.

It had failed!

All of a sudden he bounded down stairs, and through the

living room door. He pointed at me with his forefinger. 'How much money do you think you are going to send home each month?' he asked me.

The resident nurse's salary was only £8 a month. They were always hard up. They would take left over food, tea milk and sugar off the wards. They took soap and toothpaste from the lockers of the patients who had died. They stayed in at the end of the month, because they had not got the bus fare into town.

I could not hesitate for long. He was waiting for my reply.

'Three pounds,' I told him. I knew I could not manage if I offered more.

'Well,' he said slowly – 'You can take your three pounds – and blow!'

He went out of the front door, where my mother was waiting for him, and together they walked down the road.

I was free! He had told me to go!

But I knew my dad better than that!


In my small room, I spent the evening packing an old brown suitcase. It was cracked, and I tried for ages to tie the broken handle together with string. It was now under my bed.

I shivered in the coldness of the January night, as I curled up in my bed under my dad's old army coat. I listened, and waited for them to come home. Awake and fully alert, my mouth went dry when I heard them walk through the front door. I waited for him to barge into my bedroom. I waited to suffer the consequences of the scenario earlier that evening. They weren't arguing. Their voices mumbled, but quietly. I listened, without moving, as my mother came upstairs, first into the bathroom; then into their bedroom.

My dad came up next. He passed by my room. Very soon

the house was quiet. Only I was awake, wondering what the morning would bring.

The day dawned at last. I was ready for the showdown. Dad got up for work. Within half an hour, he was leaving the house. He revved up his motorbike a few extra times in the icy cold air. I listened with relieve to his bike spluttering along the avenue.

He'd gone! Without saying a word to me – he'd gone!

I dragged the old suitcase from under the bed, and quickly started to put my extra bits and pieces into it. He was sure to come back. I wanted to be as quick as possible, and out of the house. In the cold, I dressed in haste. In the kitchen, I brewed myself a cup of tea, and took it into the living room. There on the sideboard was placed a huge piece of cardboard. It couldn't be missed. Across it, hastily scribbled words that read –

'Joyce

You cannot leave this house, until I get a personal letter from matron, to say she will be personally responsible for you until the day you are 21.

Dad.'

My heart sank! No way was matron going to be personally responsible for me – to please him.

To hell with him! I was going!

I folded the large crude sheet of cardboard, and laid it across the case on top of my clothes. By this time my mother and sisters had got up and come downstairs. My sisters asked me if I was going. I hated leaving them. They would suffer. They would lie in bed, and cover their young ears to abuse and obscene language little girls should not hear. But they had each other. They would always have each other.

212

I put on my outdoor uniform coat and hat. I struggled downstairs with the battered and broken suitcase. I turned to my mother. 'I'm going now,' I said. If only she could have come to me and put her arms around me. She looked at me, and said nothing.

My sisters walked with me in the freezing fog to the bus stop. They helped me with the suitcase. I waved to them from the bus window, and watched them walk out of my life into the cold thin air, clinging to each other.

# CHAPTER TWENTY ONE

Arriving at the nurse's home, Miss Stuart, the home sister, greeted me in her lilting scotch voice. 'Before I can allocate a room to you, nurse, you have to go down to the hospital, as matron wants to see you.' I told myself I knew what had happened. My dad would be in matron's office. He would demand I went back home.

Matron was out of her office. I had a long wait in the corridor outside of her door. I was viewed quizzically by hospital staff who passed me, as I stood with the folded piece of cardboard under my arm, that contained my dad's message to me.

Matron also gave me a quizzical look as she approached in her dark green slim fitting dress and frilly white cap. She was not over friendly with her nurses, but fair. In the office I told her my story of the last twenty four hours, and showed to her the sheet of cardboard. She looked very serious.

'I take responsibility for all the girls in my care,' she said. 'You may go to the nurse's home now.'

'Thank you, Matron.'

Standing back in the corridor, still in charge of my piece of cardboard, I realized I had lots of questions I wanted to ask her. Would she write to my dad to tell him what she had just told me? Would she be able to deal with him if he came to the hospital? Would he be allowed to come into the nurse's home? It was all left unanswered, as I made my way back to the nurse's home through the snow.

Miss Stuart took me up on the lift to the third floor, the

attic bedrooms. 'I can only give you an attic room at the moment, nurse. As soon as I have another empty room I will move you.'

She unlocked the door to the tiny dark bedroom. Switching on the dim light, she showed to me the single bed, made up with plain clean linen. A bedside table held a small lamp. Dressing table, wardrobe, and a blue wicker chair left little room for anything else. A square worn rug covered the bare floor. The window was high. I felt the cool draught blowing through it.

'You know where the bathrooms are, nurse. Don't lose your door key. Goodnight now!'

'Goodnight, Sister! Thank you!'

She handed me the key to my room, and left. Closing the door behind her, I turned and looked around me. It was dim, bare, and cold. I switched on my bedside lamp that gave a warm glow to the new scene. I opened and shut the drawers, and the wardrobe that had recently been cleaned out and disinfected. I dragged the tattered brown suitcase from near the door where I had placed it, and heaved it onto the bed. It wasn't locked. It hadn't got a lock. I snapped it open, and the lid fell back. The first thing I saw lying on top of my worldly goods, was a pair of brown fur gloves. My young sister had been given them, for Christmas. They had been a very special gift, as her small delicate hands had given her much pain over the years, due to the eczema on her fingers. She had placed them in the case without me knowing. My kind little sister! I picked them up, holding them to my cheeks. My tears flowed on to them, wetting the fur.

I could not let them go, as I dragged the blue chair by my bed, to the window. I stood on the chair to look at the town below in the valley. My town! The town where I was born!

The only town I knew, where the lights were now flickering among the snowflakes on this dark Saturday afternoon.

Between my tears I looked down on the scene that illuminated the young years of my life.

I was grateful to my grandma for having loved me, for teaching me to read, to speak nicely, for wanting me to be 'a lady' when I grew up.

I was sorry for my mother. She couldn't love me. I wish she could have put her arms around me – even touched me.

I loved my dad, but did not like him.

If -I'd have had a fairy godmother, she would have tapped me on the shoulder and whispered –

'Dry your tears, my dear. Never let the past spoil the present. You are free now. Not far from you is the young man I told you of. The one you will fall head over heels in love with. The young man with dark hair and the gorgeous smile. The one you will marry in the Cathedral, in your white lace gown and flowing veil. You will have three lovely children. Dry your tears!

You have a lot to do! Maybe I should have helped you to choose another career, something more creative – but we shall see.

What of Tom and Annie? No my dear – You will never go back to them. They will attend your wedding, but not pay a penny piece towards it. Your mother will never be close to you. Forgive her! Your father will love you, and in his old age will tell you so.

Come now. Dry those tears. Do not dwell too much on your childhood. Why! – One day you may even write a book about it!'

I got down from the chair and unpacked my few

belongings from the battered case…